Chiara Lubich
On The Holy Journey

Chiara Lubich

On The
Holy Journey

New City Press

Published in the United States by New City Press
the Publishing House of the Focolare
206 Skillman Avenue, Brooklyn, New York 11211
©1988 New City Press, New York

Translated by Jerry Hearne
from the original Italian edition
In Cammino Con Il Risorto
©1987 Città Nuova Editrice, Rome, Italy

Cover design by Nick Cianfarani
ISBN 0-911782-60-5
Library of Congress Catalog Number: 88-61198
Printed in the United States of America

Nihil Obstat: Monsignor Otto L. Garcia,
Delegated Censor
Imprimatur: Francis J. Mugavero, D.D.,
Bishop of Brooklyn
Brooklyn, N.Y., June, 1988

Scripture quotations are from the *New American Bible*.
©1970 Confraternity of Christian Doctrine
Washington, D. C.

Contents

Introduction 7
Be Fire Because You Are Members of the Focolare ... 11
An Immediate Answer: Preferential Love for Jesus Forsaken 14
To Perform Even Greater Works 16
Mary, Our Model 19
Save and Return 21
To Refine the Figure of Christ in Us 24
A Divine Adventure 27
To Love Our Own Cross 29
A Directive from the Pope: "Grow and Multiply" 32
Let's Learn to be People of Prayer 35
To Work with Perfection and with Love 38
An Old, But New Commandment................. 41
Charity Means to Die, Not Just Being Ready to Die .. 43
Charity is What Counts, Charity is What Remains.... 46
To Take the Initiative 49
To Walk in the Way of Love with Love as Our Ever Present Companion 52
Our Specific Road to Sanctity 54
To Descend in order to Rise 57
To Walk with Jesus Forsaken 60
Keep On Playing 61
Building the Work of Mary Through the Communion of Goods 64
To Die Rather Than not Love You Forsaken 67
How to be Another Mary 70
How Mary Becomes Our Mother 73
Through Self-Denial We Allow the Holy Spirit to Act More Freely 76
To Be Charged with Love 79
Pray like Angels, Work like Laborers.............. 82

"I Feel Very Happy" 85
Being a Gift of Ourselves in order to Be 88
"Fully Present" 91
To Improve 94
To Overcome 97
Let's Keep Jesus in our Midst 100
Listen to the Voice of the Holy Spirit 103
To Grow and to be Overabundant 105
The Experience of God 108
To Be His Witnesses 111
100% 114
To Be Vigilant 117
Perfect Works out of Love for Jesus Forsaken 119
To Be Reborn through Love 122
Unceasing Love for Him 125
To Follow Jesus 128
Mary, a Molder of Saints 131
To Love without Holding Back 134
Choose Jesus Forsaken in order to be Fit for the Kingdom of God 137
Look at Jesus Forsaken and You Will Find the Answer 140
Call Him by Name 142
Giving Joy to Heaven 144
Spending the Day with Mary 146
The Lifestyle of the Work of Mary is Love 149
Live the Present to Perfection 151
Renewing Reciprocal Love 154
The Necessary Attributes for Those who Want to Undertake a Holy Journey 156
Who is the Layperson for the Church 159
Christmas with Those who Suffer 162

Introduction

The writings in this book reflect some of the advancements achieved in Christian spirituality today. Their true dimension and value can be better appreciated by understanding their origin. The texts are products of a collective spirituality. They focus on the rediscovery of all Christian values, especially communitarian ones. Every spirituality of the Church is built upon a specific aspect of the Gospel. The spirituality explained in this text, which is the spirituality of the Focolare, known officially as the Work of Mary, is built on the aspect of unity. Its foundation lies in going to God through one's neighbor. This is in accord with what Pope John Paul II writes in his encyclical *Redemptor Hominis:* "Man is the primary and principle road of the Church."

This book is not a series of personal reflections centering on one particular topic. It is a collection of the thoughts of Chiara Lubich, foundress of the Focolare, which were transmitted every two weeks to the most committed of its members throughout the world. A more complete explanation can be found in the Introduction of the book *Journey*, by the same author, of which this book is a continuation. On one side, the intention of these bi-weekly transmissions is to reach simultaneously as many people of the Focolare as possible, yet its principle focus is to live out and deepen the concept of "walking together."

What can be seen to emerge from these texts is a life lived as a "holy journey" toward Christian perfection to which Jesus invites us. ("Be perfect as your heavenly Father is perfect" Mt 5:48.) Vatican Council II has reaffirmed this as the vocation of the entire Church (cf. LG, 39).

These meditations, though brief, are incisive and profound. They are written in a spoken style, and continuously call attention to loving God with one's whole self which by its very nature includes love for neighbor. The author's insistence on love for neighbor reveals her particular understanding of St. Paul's teaching that those who love their neighbor have fulfilled the law (cf. Gal 5:14).

In different and creative ways the text points out that authentic love for God cannot but pass through the cross. In the Focolare this is expressed through love for Jesus Forsaken, the Son of God who in the height of His suffering cried out, "My God, my God, why have you forsaken me?" (Mt 27:46). Jesus in His forsakenness, at this apex of His suffering and love, is the key to unity between God and humankind, and humankind within itself. Love for Him "forsaken," which calls for love as He loved, brings about unity. Unity permits Jesus to be present in a special way in the midst of the community. ("Where two or three are gathered in my name, there am I in the midst of them" Mt 18:20.)

Many of these pages refer to the spiritual progress and steps already reached. They do not contain the full range of topics that the spirituality develops. This text draws principally on the will of God, the gifts of the Holy Spirit, Christian values, the ascent to God—all serving to contribute to enlighten and strengthen the common commitment to holiness which is the true unifying intention of each of the writings.

These writings did not follow a planned outline. They developed as the two week period given to live out each spiritual thought matured into new insights for the continuation of the "journey." There is nothing in these pages that result from abstract or pure thinking. They represent the life lived by a vast group of people who follow the spirituality of unity. It is interesting to see how from the joyful and painful events of daily life, new motivation can be found for attaining greater union with God, for prayer, and for conversion. From time to time, the topic of death appears, resulting from a close communion established with some of the members of the Focolare up until their last moments of life. The attention given to this topic is an attention of love, since the spirituality begins on the premise of faith in the love of God. The incidents of death mentioned portray the deep level of Christian experience reached. Chiara's assertion, "Margrit has fully reconciled us with death" (cf. pp 87), seems to be another version of St. Francis' "May you be praised, my Lord, by our sister death."

The mention of union with Mary (cf. p 71) carries signs of a wider Christian experience of Mary, of a deeper union attained with her by people of all walks of life. Mary is the model for all members of the Focolare. Each time Chiara speaks of her it is not for the purpose of giving a Marian touch to spiritual life. Instead, it is to propose her once again as the *model* of spiritual life. She is the true Mother and leader of the life of the Focolare.

It is important to underline that the charism of the Focolare is love, as Pope John Paul II declared on his visit to its headquarters, called the Mariapolis Center, in Rocca di Papa, Italy (cf. p 33).

Finally, what links these writings together is that they are lived meditations on the Word of Life. One of the practices of the Focolare members is to choose a sentence of Scripture each month, taken from the liturgy, so that it can be applied to daily living. Consequently, the words of Jesus become "life."

There are occasional references made to the organization and structure of the Focolare. However, what prevails, in clarity and style, is the evangelical and ecclesial foundation upon which the author's ideas are based. Keeping in mind the wide and diverse cultural range of her readers, Chiara renders her thoughts accessible to all.

If it happens that Chiara may seem to display both admiration and awe on account of the working of the spirit of God throughout the vast spreading of the Focolare, such sentiments are also full of gratitude to Him who provides the strength for her thoughts which effectively contribute toward guiding a large number of people along the splendid road of sanctity.

The Editor

Be Fire Because You Are Members of the Focolare

The Word of Life[1] which casts light on the path of our Holy Journey this month begins in this way: "Get rid of all the old yeast to make yourselves fresh dough, unleavened loaves, as it were" (1 Cor 5:7).

We have already commented upon this Word of Life various times in the past because of the way it seemed to have caught our attention. In fact, we could also read it in this way: remove the old leaven (the leaven of evil) because you no longer have this leaven (through the grace of being Christian). It is almost like saying, "*Be* Christians because you *are* Christians." This Word of Life can be truly useful for many followers of Christ. Oftentimes, in fact, we hear the complaint: Christians exist, but are not recognized as such because they do not live as authentic Christians. Instead they should be singled out for their love, for the fire of charity they possess.

It is a Word of Life which for us could also be read like this: *be* fire because you *are* members of the Focolare.[2]

Recently I was at Via dei Cestari, near Minerva[3] where St. Catherine of Siena is buried. I remember other visits I have paid to her tomb. One during the beginnings of the Focolare in Rome when a writing of hers had deeply struck us: "If you are what you are supposed to be, you can set all of Italy on

---

[1] *The Word of Life refers to a particular passage of Scripture, to be reflected upon and lived by members of the Focolare throughout the world. It is generally accompanied by a commentary written by the author, Chiara Lubich.*
[2] *To better understand the imagery: Focolare is an Italian word meaning "hearth" or "fireplace."*
[3] *Via dei Cestari is the street in Rome where the Church of Santa Maria over Minerva is located.*

fire."⁴ With infinite gratitude I realized that this fire has been enkindled all over the world; it has at least been lit. The entire world has not yet been set ablaze during the course of these forty years, but we can say that a fire has been enkindled throughout the world. At this time I felt an immense desire within: to see this fire *burst into a blaze.*

But how can this happen?

It seemed to me that St. Catherine was repeating to me again: "If you are what you are supposed to be..." I made a connection between her invitation and the Word of Life for this month.

Are we Christians? Then, we must *be* Christians.

Are we members of the Focolare? Then, we must *be* fire. Really be fire! We know that a fire cannot be sustained unless it is fed by paper, by wood, straw or other materials. In the same way, we cannot be love unless we love. Our neighbors give us this opportunity. Since in some way we always have people around us we can be fire.

We must remember that our way to God is our neighbor. The love we feel in our hearts for God grows in as much as we love our neighbor concretely.

We are scattered all over the world. Take out a map and examine the area you live in to see to what extent the Focolare has spread. Take notice of the fire which already exists. See what kind of fire it is. It may be already burning, or just enkindled, or still gaining strength under the ashes. Take note of the places where a fire has not yet been set and then work at setting one.

If you start out by being who you are supposed to be, you will bring about the same fire in those with whom you come in contact. They in turn will do so for others and so on. Jesus wants us to set a blaze. He wants it set throughout the world.

Yes, the third Christian millennium is approaching, and it must see the fulfillment of these words: "If you are what you are supposed to be, you will set fire all over Korea, throughout Paraguay, Portugal, all over the Ivory Coast, in other words, in every nation of the world; and then in every region of every

---

⁴*St. Catherine of Siena,* Epistolario, II, *Alba 1966, p. 442.*

nation, and then in every city, in every town.

If the Focolare has reached the point that it has today, why should it not move further ahead?

It can happen if we want it. Then it will be Jesus Himself, the Risen Lord, who will enkindle this fire and spread it. He can be in our midst, He can always be in each one of us. And for this to be true, we know what He expects from us. It is enough then, that we want it.

In the next two weeks, let's keep this thought in mind: "I must be fire for all those I meet and for those who have been entrusted to me."

April 5, 1984

An Immediate Answer:
Preferential Love for Jesus Forsaken

In our last conference call we spoke about what could be called St. Catherine's project today, which has been received with great enthusiasm: "If you are what you are supposed to be, you will set the whole world on fire." From the cables and letters that I received I understood that the spiritual thought of that last conference call had touched the deepest recesses of your hearts. It aimed at the very center of our vocation which for the mercy of God and His glory calls us to great things. St. Catherine goes on to say, "Don't be satisfied with little things because God expects big things from you."[5]

Together with all of you I have tried to live according to her teaching by putting into practice that phrase which invites us to be who we are.

A few days ago I asked myself, "Who am I and who are we that we aspire to be what we should be in the fullest sense of the word?" At that moment I happened to have been passing in front of a large image of Jesus Forsaken, and immediately the answer came: we are those who have chosen You as the Ideal of our lives. "I have only one Spouse on earth, Jesus crucified and forsaken. I have no God, but Him." Then and there, as if it were a totally new idea, I remembered my preferential love for Him; that exclusive choice of Him which I have declared to Him many times. I felt a burning desire within to love Him as never before.

But how? In what way? Certainly by loving Him in everyone, but especially in those who resemble Him the most; those who suffer in any particular way, those who seem to us to be farthest from God; then in the little children and in the young people today who are exposed to the deadly

---

[5] *Ibid.* III, p. 138.

atmosphere of indifference, atheism, and immorality, to say the least. Indeed, if our revolution has taken on a special thrust, as in these past few days it seems to me it has; if we look at our little map showing the spreading of the Focolare in the particular area which has been entrusted to us; if we have in our hands or if we are in the process of compiling the lists of persons whom we are responsible for in a special way; then we should give the place of honor to those who remind us most of Jesus Forsaken. We have to dedicate our primary attention and the available time that we have for them. By following this procedure, I am sure that everything else will fall into place. This is the best approach for being what we are supposed to be. We should be similar to Jesus who came for the sick, and not for the healthy; for sinners, not for the righteous. The healthy and the righteous will follow along on their own.

Tomorrow, Good Friday, is a great feast day of ours, a feast of suffering and love. Let the kissing of the cross this year symbolize the sealing of our promise to love Him throughout the coming year in those who remind us most of Him, in those who resemble Him the most.

Meanwhile for today, Holy Thursday, let's keep in mind the new Commandment of which He is the measure, the prayer for unity to which He is the key, and the Eucharist in which He gives us Himself—body, soul and divinity—in the very mystery of His Passion. Let us also remember the priesthood which in Jesus finds its fulfillment in the abandonment on the cross.

Let's all remain immersed in these immense mysteries which are our life and joy.

April 19, 1984

To Perform Even Greater Works

The Word of Life of the month of May invites us to believe in Jesus in order to accomplish works similar to His and to perform even greater ones (cf. Jn 14:12). How can ordinary creatures like ourselves arrive at such a state of being?

The works that Jesus refers to are those which concern the redemption and the salvation of humankind.

But since Jesus had already fully redeemed the world through His death, resurrection and ascension into Heaven; He would then act fully on behalf of the world, not directly, but through other people.

Thus He spread the faith throughout the world by means of His disciples. The works that He has accomplished and still accomplishes today through the lives of others can be greater works than those He Himself performed while on earth, because they hold the effects of a redemption that has been fully achieved. However, it is not the people themselves who perform these works similar to His or even greater, even though their own cooperation is needed. It is Jesus who dwells in them, the one who performs them.

Persons who feel capable on their own of accomplishing works similar to those of Jesus are like children, who because they are in the arms of their father, think they are as tall as he is. Those who feel capable of performing even greater works than He are like the same children, who seated atop the shoulders of their father think they are even taller than he is because they can now reach up and touch the ceiling. Children can certainly reach the height of their father and even higher, but it is because they are carried by him.

So it is for Christians. The Risen Lord lives in them. If Christians allow Him to live, they can accomplish works worthy of Him; works similar to those of Jesus before He died, and even greater ones.

What do we need to do in order that the Risen Lord may live in us?

We know what the answer is. Upon rising in the morning, we must immediately point our compasses toward Jesus Forsaken, telling Him "here I am," and then be faithful to Him throughout the day. In other words: to love suffering.

St. John of the Cross, who reached the heights of sanctity, and who therefore completed his Holy Journey with the greatest of success, was asked why so few reach such heights of union with God. He responded that it is because instead of loving suffering, people seek consolation, while those who do love suffering know what it means to live with the Risen Lord within: it is a foretaste of Heaven.

If this, then, is the way things stand, let's try during the next two weeks to give the sufferings that we may encounter each day their fullest value. Not so much the sufferings that are a product of our own imagination, but the sufferings offered to us by the will of God: uncomfortable circumstances, neighbors to love fully to the end, the necessary mortifications so often implied for us who must live in this world, but certainly not of this world.

Besides, we have a great need to allow the Risen Lord to live within us. Our goal, in fact, is to accomplish an immense task: to light up the fire of charity in the world, beginning with our own environments. The objective that we must strive for is not an easy one, but a difficult one: to love those far from God, as Jesus had done.

The Risen Lord then, in simple terms, must shine forth within and among us.

In order for this to happen, we must, as we say, live "beyond the wound of Jesus Forsaken."[6] In this way our charity will always be aflame, and our living quarters or meeting places will be like fires, whether they be the focolare centers, or the homes of a family-focolare, or a nucleus of Voluteers, a Gen unit, a religious community, or a *grappolo*

---

[6]*This saying used by the Focolare expresses the desire to not remain crushed by suffering, but to love suffering through love for Jesus in the wound of His forsakenness. The author gives a further explanation in: Chiara Lubich,* Unity and Jesus Forsaken, *New York, 1985, pp. 70-71.*

meeting.[7] They will all be aflame with love bearing all the consequences that one could imagine along the lines of *ut omnes* (that all may be one). All the same, we shouldn't be astonished to see that our field of action extends throughout the whole world while Jesus had remained only within the confines of Palestine. We will have the certainty that it is always He who acts. Nor should we be surprised to see a greater number of conversions springing forth through us, than those brought about through Jesus. It is always He who converts.

Let's remember that there can be no flame, fire or blaze without combustible material. This material is our ego which must burn, even though it would always want to prevail. But when we embrace difficult moments with love, our ego will die out, and upon its death, the life of Jesus in us will be in continual resurrection.

Therefore, let's fill these next two weeks with many examples of concrete love for Jesus Forsaken.

May 3, 1984

---

[7] The term grappolo, *Italian for a cluster of grapes, is used to define a group of persons who are linked with one another on their common journey of sanctification. A further explanation can be found in: Chiara Lubich,* Journey, *New York, 1986, p. 30.*

Mary, Our Model

We have now come to the latter half of the month of May. It is a month, in part because of the blossoming of spring, at least in our area, and above all because it is a month dedicated to Mary, that we cannot but feel overtaken by a wave of tenderness, sweetness, and a special love for our most amiable Mother. After having heard the Holy Father cry out his prayer, entrusting the world to her Immaculate Heart, I would expect that we as members of the Work of Mary would not allow this month to pass by without having personally consecrated ourselves to her, without having pronounced a *totus tuus*[8] from deep within our hearts, so that on her part she may be able to entrust us in the greatest way she can to Jesus.

For the very fact that we are members of the Focolare, we must develop a very close relationship with Our Lady. It is not only we who are conscious of this. Others who lovingly follow the course of our work have also noticed this. We have even had this confirmed in these past few days.

As you can imagine, the Holy Father on his recent trip to the Far East often encountered Focolarini, Gen, Volunteers and priests, etc. Their presence, which appeared so universally, caused a member of the Holy Father's staff to inquire, "But how do you manage to be so present everywhere?" Another responded on our behalf, "It's the work of Mary. It is Mary!" That person was probably referring to the richness of fruits that Mary and her Works bring about, but this answer gave us great joy for still another reason.

As we all know, Mary, our most amiable Mother, is our Ideal, our model; she is our "form." Mary, as we say, is what

---

[8]*Latin meaning "all Yours," a phrase used by Pope John Paul II to express his personal dedication to Mary.*

we "should be." In our turn, we are those who "can be" like her.

When we experience moments of fulfillment (which occur when the Risen Lord shines forth within us through the death of our ego), and then see ourselves from a supernatural point of view, we discover ourselves to be, in a certain way, another little Mary. In fact, it is she who is our fulfillment.

Remember the prayer that we formulated many years ago, in asking Jesus why it could have been that He, who wanted to remain present on all parts of the earth in the Eucharist, did not find a way to leave behind the presence of His Mother so that she too might help us on our journey through life?

Remember the answer that I perceived within my heart: "It is because I want to see her in you; even though you are not immaculate, my love will make you whole."

My hope, therefore, is that today, after many years, Jesus can look down from Heaven to all parts of the earth and in some way see in many of us, at least in certain moments, the image of His Mother; and that He be comforted by the fact, should this be true, that Mary, through our lives, can continue to open her heart and her arms to a suffering humanity, especially to those far from God.

With this hope in mind, an immense gratitude fills my heart and must also fill yours, together with the ardent resolution made to Jesus: "To die rather than not love You forsaken." It is through meeting Jesus Forsaken, as the words of an early song of ours tell us, that we can become another Mary.

During the next two weeks, then, faced with each difficulty that arises before us, or that we may encounter in living the virtues, above all charity, we must continually repeat: "To die, rather than not love You forsaken." Living in this way, we will also give joy to Mary. In seeing on this earth sons and daughters in some way similar to her, imagine what graces she will give us, transforming our earthly life into a continual springtime.

May 17, 1984

Save and Return

A few days have gone by since we have left behind us, with a certain sense of nostalgia, the month of May which carries such fascination. However, the month of June, filled with many important feasts, has now opened before us and awakens deep sentiments within us. We celebrated the feast of the Ascension on the third, with the extraordinary meeting held by our New Humanity and Youth for a United World movements.[9] In three days we will celebrate Pentecost. Following will be the feast of the Most Holy Trinity, then the feast of the Most Sacred Body and Blood of Jesus, and finally the feast of the Immaculate Heart of Mary. These feast days represent such Heavenly realities and are so part of our lives, that they seem too numerous to meditate upon and fully appreciate in the short span of one month.

Let's focus a moment on the feast that will arrive in three days, perhaps just in time to prepare ourselves a bit. Pentecost, which celebrates the extraordinary descent of the Holy Spirit—fruit of the death of Jesus—upon Mary, the Apostles and the early Christian community. It is a feast day for which we always experienced an intimate affinity, perhaps not even knowing why, or perhaps for an association made between the ideas that the flames of the Focolare represent and the flames which descended within the Cenacle.

Yes, perhaps for this reason. Do you remember that even Pope John Paul II drew a link between these two ideas when he spoke at our Genfest in 1980? "...the Focolare," he said, "a term which holds great significance for you. A thought takes us spontaneously back to the first 'Focolare' formed by

---

[9] *An international meeting sponsored by two of the branches of the Focolare called the New Humanity Movement and Youth For a United World. The meeting, whose topic was "Economy and Work," was held at the Ergife Hotel in Rome on June 3, 1984.*

the disciples gathered together in the Cenacle...."

Pentecost: therefore, the Holy Spirit, the Focolare.

We must celebrate the reoccurrence of this feast of Pentecost in the best possible way, for the gratitude which we cannot but feel toward the Third Divine Person of the Most Holy Trinity, who has so lavished us with gifts to the point of changing our lives.

How can we celebrate this feast?

I see no other way than by reviving the flame that was given to each one of us: I, my own, each one of you, your own: our flame of love.

The Word of Life for this month can be of significant help to us. Jesus says, "God did not send the Son into the world to condemn the world, but so that the world may be saved through Him" (Jn 3:17). It is the revelation of the purpose of Jesus' life: He came into this world in order to save, in order to live His name: Savior.

This passage of Jesus instills two attitudes within us. Foremost, it makes us see in each neighbor, someone who must not be condemned but be saved.

It also makes us look at ourselves as persons loved by God, no matter what our situation; persons who can always return to His infinite mercy.

This Word of Life teaches us how to live as if we are already in Heaven where there is more rejoicing over a sinner who returns than for ninety-nine who are righteous. It helps us not to judge or to condemn, but to love always, always ready to save. It is a Word of Life which draws us toward those who are far from God, giving Heaven the joy of an eventual moment of festivity.

This Word of Life also urges us to always return to God, which means to continually begin again; it encourages us to nourish our inner flame of charity with His mercy.

It is logical that these attitudes imply a certain cost. It is not easy to be always ready to forgive and to save. It is much easier to allow ourselves to become judgmental. We must so frequently exercise understanding and forgiveness towards others that it becomes a habit.

Equally so, it is not always easy to entrust our own selves to God's mercy. The weight of our mistakes can more easily cause us to get discouraged, but we must return to Him just the same, reminding ourselves that He has come also to save us. We reestablish our rapport with God when we allow ourselves to be immersed in His mercy. We then experience a renewed union with God, more so then when we count solely on our own personal strength and believe that we are making good progress without His help.

Therefore, what motto can we choose for these next two weeks in order that our lives may be a living celebration of Pentecost? Two words: *save and return*. To save the others; and as for ourselves, to always turn back to God, to begin again.

In this way, we will certainly live the feast of the Most Holy Trinity.

We will be in touch again prior to the arrival of the feasts which will follow.

May the Father, Son, and Holy Spirit enfold us all in their infinite love.

June 7, 1984

To Refine the Figure of Christ in Us

We continue on our life's Holy Journey. There are some who have already completed their journey, and some who have just recently joined us. The predominant feature of this journey is our thrust toward sanctity which is the task of every Christian. Along with you, I am also trying each day to keep the pace, and anchored in prayer in order to obtain the grace of God, I forge ahead.

For this reason, I took a little book along with me on my trip to Istanbul, a book which offers wonderful suggestions in this regard: it is called *Imitation of Christ,* recently edited and published by *Città Nuova* publications. Although these writings are directed toward those dedicated to Jesus through an individual path in which a person journeys to God alone, a path different from our own, yet, they provide useful suggestions, full of wisdom and experience, for us who travel toward God in a more collective fashion.

Its keynote is to emphasize the importance of the virtues.

You all know how in acquiring these virtues and in struggling against their opposing vices, we, who are called by God to find our "fortune" through our neighbor, discover self-denial of our selves through our very love for Him. You know that to improve ourselves, it is not within our practice to aim directly at our defects, but instead, to go around these obstacles by "changing room," as we say, or by "living the others." In doing so, we place ourselves in the way of charity which is the source of every virtue.

All the same, our Statutes do underline the task of exercising the virtues. It is our task, the more we progress along our spiritual journey, to take them into consideration.

Besides, it is Jesus Forsaken who is the model of all virtues, to whom we have given our lives. We always say that we want to love Him not only in suffering, but also in the practice of the virtues.

Charity, in fact, carves out the figure of Christ in us; when we love, we are another Christ. However, loving Jesus Forsaken in the practice of the virtues gives us the impression of refining that sculpture, of giving it the finishing touches.

Notwithstanding our love for our neighbors, we still carry along our little defects, even the smallest ones, which take something away from the beauty of Christ within us. Because of this, we are often dissatisfied with ourselves; though conscious of our great efforts, we are still humiliated by our own personal imperfections.

Which defects are these? Everyone has their own. At times our actions suffer due to our haste, or to our imperfection in carrying out the will of God; we may get distracted in our prayer, or pay too much attention to the foolish things that the world likes; perhaps we lose control over our appetite. We may be often overcome by curiosity, or fall into pride. We may tend to speak needlessly, or without thinking of what we are saying. We can be attached to little things, somewhat dependent on the use of television. We allow ourselves to seek to be served by the others; we become inconsistent, and so on.

What should we do in this case?

When it is a question of things that are not good, Jesus invites us to act with decision when he affirms: If your eye is a cause for scandal, than take it out. (cf. Mt 5:29)

Therefore, out of love for Jesus Forsaken, not wavering, but remaining who we are, we must still uproot our vices, one after another, even while continuing along our own path, which is the path of love.

The *Imitation of Christ* tells us that it is not easy. In fact, it states that if we free ourselves from one vice each year, we will become perfect in a short time.

I am convinced that this is made even more possible through our own spiritual path. Love in fact is very helpful for this. Love is the denial of self, and burns our defects away.

Just the same, it would not be a bad idea to aim at one of our defects by creating a habit of practicing its opposing virtue.

Let's take courage then and go to work!

Let's continue to love, and until our next encounter, let's

create a habit of practicing the virtues that are the opposites of at least three of our defects.

Our Lady will assist us. She knows that we want to offer her the gift of our sanctification. Athletes, at times, undergo strenuous training in order to excel in an endeavor which is solely human. Let's find ourselves exerting at least as much effort.

May our love for Jesus Forsaken, whom we also encounter in the struggle to possess the virtues, obtain its greatest possible victory.

June 21, 1984

A Divine Adventure

It may be possible that some of us may have forgotten about a reality that was ever present in the early days of the Focolare, and which the Word of Life this month places before us. If we love God, life and our own life itself with all of its many circumstances becomes a divine adventure in which there is no moment lacking which does not astonish us for the newness it brings. A divine adventure full of treasures to be discovered, to be enriched from moment to moment. A continual placing of little ceramic tiles into the mosaic of our sanctity.

The Word of Life this month tells us. "We know that in all things God works for good with those who love Him" (Rom 8:28). *In all things*... with those who love Him. All things. Nothing—and we must believe this—happens by chance. No joyful occasion, or indifferent or sorrowful one, no encounter, no family, work, or school situation, no condition of physical or moral health, is without meaning. Instead, all things, events, situations, and persons, are bearers of a message on the part of God, which we must know how to read and to accept with all our heart.

All things work for the good, for those who love God. God has His own design of love for each one of us. He loves us with a personal love, and—if we believe in this love and respond with our own love (here the condition!)—He brings all things toward the fulfillment of His plan for us.

It is enough to look at Jesus. We know how much He loved the Father. If we think for a moment of only Him, we can see how, during the whole arc of His life, He fully lived the Word of Life for this month. For Him nothing happened by chance. Everything had a purpose.

However, we see this Word personified in Him in a unique way during the last days of His life; nothing regarding His passion and death happened by chance.

For Him, even the extreme trial of the abandonment of the Father cooperated toward the good, because in overcoming this trial, He brought His Work to completion.

The causes of His passion were perhaps blind ones. Those who made Him suffer and die did not know what they were doing. They did not know whom they tortured and crucified. They were not aware of conducting a sacrifice, the sacrifice par excellance, that would bring about the salvation of humanity. Jesus was made to suffer by persons who acted without this intention in mind, but since He loved the Father, He transformed all these things into means of redemption, seeing in those terrible moments, the hour so long awaited, the fulfillment of His divine, earthly adventure.

Jesus' example must enlighten our own life: everything that comes to us, all that happens, all that surrounds us and all that causes us to suffer, must be understood as the will of God, who loves us, or to be understood as permitted by Him, who loves us still.

Everything will take on a new meaning; everything will have a purpose; everything will be extremely useful.

Let's take heart. Our lives are still before us. We are still on our journey. Life can still be transformed into a divine adventure. The plan of God for us can still be fulfilled. It's enough to continue loving and keep our eyes open toward His ever splendid will.

August 2, 1984

To Love Our Own Cross

I would also like to talk to you at this time about the Word of Life, referring back to our last conference call in order to examine again the possibility of transforming our life into a divine adventure.

Why do I speak to you about this? I feel it is a topic of great importance. I can see, above all in the lives of the first Focolarini and Focolarine who through the grace of God have made the effort to live in this way since the early days of the Focolare, the extraordinary result reached in abandoning oneself completely to God, and in allowing Him to reveal to us day by day the steps to be taken in order to fulfill His plan for each one of us.

This divine adventure produced the following result for us: we witnessed a new, modern Work of God of concrete significance emerge in the world; we saw it plant its roots deeply into the Church's soil. We admired throughout the years, the spreading of its branches to the ends of the earth.

Imagine, in the diversity of the unique plans of God for each person, what it would be like if everyone in the world made the effort to let their lives be shaped by Him? Certainly, the face of the earth would be soon renewed. In any case, these thoughts serve to encourage us not to fall short in our own personal commitment. Therefore let's take another look at what our part should be so that the remainder of our life can be transformed into a divine adventure. Everything works for the good... everything, therefore, serves its purpose for the good. "All things God works for good [but] with those who love Him." To love God! We certainly do want to love Him. But, when are we sure that we are loving Him? It is not only when we give our hearts to Him in a moment when everything is going for the better, because that would be easy, and beautiful, but could also be just an enthusiastic reaction or one mixed with personal interest or love for ourselves, and not for Him. We can be certain we love Him if we do so also in adverse situations; furthermore, to guarantee true love for Him, we have decided to prefer Him, above all, in everything that hurts us. To love God in our obstacles and in our pains is always true, sure love. We express this kind of love with the words: to love Jesus crucified and forsaken.

To transform our lives, then, into a divine adventure, and to have the certainty that all of the past, present and future of our lives is directly useful toward fulfilling the plan of God for each of us, requires a choice of Jesus Forsaken.

But which cross, which Jesus Forsaken, must we desire to love? Certainly not a vague cross, as if to say: I want to make my own, the crosses of the Focolare and the sufferings of humanity. Not the cross which can be a product of our imagination; for example, dreams of a martyrdom that may never come about.

To be His follower, Jesus said, "Whoever wants to come after me must take up his cross" (cf. Lk 9:23). *His* personal cross! Therefore, everyone must love their own cross, their *own* Jesus Forsaken.

If, in fact, at a certain moment of our lives, Jesus had appeared before us and in the power of His love had asked us to follow Him, to choose Him, to—as if to say—espouse Him, He didn't intend to manifest Himself to us in just a vague way, but instead a very precise way. He asked us to embrace Him in all those pains, worries, sicknesses, temptations, in those situations, persons and responsibilities that touch our very person, to the point of being able to say: "This is *my* cross," or even better, "This is *my* Spouse!" All of us have our own personal Jesus Forsaken, which is not the one of our neighbor, nor of anyone else; but really our own.

Therefore, if we learn to read beyond the trauma of our various personal sufferings, and see the love of God for each of us, life becomes magnificent, and draws us to be ever closer to our Jesus Forsaken, to embrace Him, as the saints have done, and to yearn to see Him transformed in us in a resurrection personally related to our very selves, since "Jesus" in me is also distinct from "Jesus" in my neighbor.

What is our next step?

In order not to lose any time, each of us can make a brief examination of his or her own present situation, and then decide, with the help of God, to say yes to all those things for which we would want to cry out otherwise, but know are the will of God.

If we live in this way, everything will take on a deeper meaning. At times we will be like the grain of wheat which, because it knows how to die, will see its shoots spring forth. At times like the branch, which allows itself to be pruned, we will later see the choicest fruits.

During these next two weeks, let's rise in the morning with this sense of determination: "I will live today for the sole purpose of loving *my* Jesus Forsaken."

Everything else will fall into place. The Risen Lord will live in each of us and among us. He will extend His Work of Mary out to new horizons, for His own glory and the glory of Mary and for the purposes that Heaven knows, and we can perceive He will give us happiness already here on earth.

August 16, 1984

A Directive from the Pope: "Grow and Multiply"

We still bear a very special joy in our hearts for the Holy Father's visit to the headquarters of the Focolare and for our gratitude to Mary who, on the feast of the Assumption—we seem to feel—had hinted that suggestion to him.

It was an extraordinary event. Not only for the Holy Father, who defined it as such for the message it had carried. But—as you can imagine—it was above all an extraordinary event for us.

Everything at our headquarters now seems to be blessed and even more so. The Holy Father met with the Coordinating Council and its various members, and has become acquainted with the sixty houses and apartments that constitute the Mariapolis in the vicinity of Rome. In it he sees, in miniature, an image of the very nature of the Church.

In fact, through the presence of laypersons consecrated in various ways, the presence of young people, of families, of people committed in society, of priests, religious and sisters; through the presence of its various activities and for its work for the principal goals of the Church, the Holy Father sees in the Work of Mary not only a component of the Church, but the very features of the Church as it has defined itself in the Second Vatican Council.

The entire Focolare now appears to us to be more than blessed. The Pope said he was aware of the unity which binds us all together and addressed himself to all of you throughout the world.

And now that the entire Work of Mary has received this copious blessing on the part of Heaven through the Vicar of Christ on earth, a sense of urgency compels us to the deep desire of performing everything well, to keep charity alive in all, to pray better, much better, and to maintain our homes and possessions clean and orderly, our offices functioning properly, and so on.

The Holy Father has also recognized the solidity of the Focolare in all its particular details, and did not feel the need to offer any particular direction. Yet, because he was so fascinated — we feel — by the beauty of the Work of Mary, a directive for us did flow out from his heart: "Grow and multiply."

These are the words that we will try to put into practice in the best possible way beginning with the next two weeks.

To grow: we can do this by living out our splendid ideal which is — as the Holy Father said — love, the totality of love. It is a love which does not allow for disunity, division, or hate; but overcomes all things, since it is stronger than all else. We know that we can find this radicality in our contemplation and love for Jesus Forsaken, the highest expression and example of the greatest love.

And to multiply: How? Let's consider for a moment our various responsibilities, in particular the persons entrusted to us and the communities to whom we dedicate our efforts. Let's assess what needs to be done, and give of ourselves without measure according to the norms of our Ideal, with the faith that God can act even when we are unable to ourselves. Let's take a look at our maps,[10] the ones that we showed to the Holy Father. Examine to what point we have arrived, and where the Focolare has not yet been developed; where knots are missing along the net of *ut omnes* (that all may be one). Let's be sure that the development accounted for in our zones, the revolution of love that gave such hope to the Holy Father, is actually alive and moving forward, particularly in the area specifically entrusted to us.

"Grow and multiply." We know that these two realities are linked to one another: the more we grow within, the more we increase in numbers, because we love more. But we can also say: the more we increase in numbers, the more the love of God grows within us.

With this in mind, let's go forward, keeping our eyes on Mary, our leader.

---

[10] *The maps which indicate the spreading of the Focolare throughout the world.*

Our divine adventure continues. We should fall on our knees in adoration of God for the love He has shown us. And in this sweet and solemn moment, let's not forget those who have gone before us, who worked and suffered and passed on to the Next Life offering their lives for the Focolare. May the Holy Spirit join all of us from both the earthly and heavenly Mariapolis into a single hymn of thanksgiving and in the solemn determination to always do everything better.

Remember: "Grow and multiply."

September 6, 1984

Let's Learn to be People of Prayer

Urged on in these last two weeks by the encouraging words of the Holy Father, we have tried to carry out his directive: "Grow and multiply." Today we would like to take a look at the Word of Life for this month to see how it can also help us to accomplish this. The passage reads, "What profit would a man show if he were to gain the whole world and destroy himself in the process?" (Mt 16:26).

Through its commentary, we know what Jesus intended by these words. For us, who are members of the Work of Mary, this passage has the following significance: What profit can you show by allowing yourselves, at times, to be drawn into such frenzied apostolic activity, into what could be called almost a "heresy of action," which practically absorbs all your time, when instead, it is the will of God for you to grow in many other ways? What importance does it have to be so committed to bringing to God many souls when your own soul remains small and imperfect, because for example, it will not search out a truly peaceful moment to be so needfully nourished by prayer? What importance does all this have, when the very prayers that are a sacred duty for you are performed in the midst of endless distractions and recited only superficially, hurriedly or have become shortened in length?

Certainly, for those who may find themselves in this state of existence, this Word of Life is the best corrective to reinstill the right disposition to grow within; it can reawaken the need to live for the *porro unum* ("one thing only is required," cf. Lk 10:42) and that is union with God.

Moreover, the Word of Life for this month redirects us on the right path to live out our apostolate, our task: to multiply. In fact, this should not be basically anything other than the irradiation of our love for God.

But if our love weakens, since there can be no union with

God without prayer, what can we possibly irradiate?

Therefore, prayer! In these next two weeks let's examine our prayer life and allow it to emerge forth in those moments set aside during the day, and in those moments when we spontaneously seek God. They are the luminous background of our love for God in all that we do.

What can we do in order for this to come about?

First of all, when we prepare monthly, weekly and daily schedules, let's include time for prayer.

Then, let's try not to overtire ourselves prior to these moments so as not to arrive before God without the strength and the capability to concentrate, and so as not to feel compelled to provide for Him only the less joyful moments of our day.

Let's be sure to always precede our prayer with a moment of recollection.

Then, let's pray from our hearts, and unite our souls to what we pronounce in words.

We already have spoken about the need of prayer that asks for God's graces so as not to lean solely on our own strength.

During these next two weeks, let's take a look at all of our prayers: even those through which we adore God, and praise Him, and ask Him forgiveness for ourselves and for everyone, and also the prayers in which we express our thanksgiving.

Let's examine whether our meditation or our "going into depth" is done in the best possible way. Let's perfect our morning and evening prayers; the prayers we say during our visit to the Most Holy Sacrament. Let's see how well we pray the rosary. Above all, lets take a look at daily mass and the way we receive the Eucharist.

If everything is done well, there would certainly be nourishment for our soul! Let's not waste this opportunity as if it were something merely secondary, which does not merit all our attention. Let's pray in unity with others when it is possible, so that our prayers may gain strength. And then let's also pray in the secret of our rooms, as the Gospel wishes us to.

Since these times are certainly not times in which those who pray in public run the risk of falling into pride because they are praised by others, let's also, when it is the right moment, manifest our faith to the world. We can do this by returning to the practice of making the sign of the cross while passing in front of a church, or other sacred places; before meals, even at a restaurant; at the beginning of a trip by train, car or plane, so that in doing so we might call to the attention of those most distracted what is of most value.

To sum up, let's learn to be true persons of prayer and to offer to God all that we do during the day, so as to transform also our activities into prayer.

In this way, everything will go better. Our Holy Journey will have the fuel it needs.

If it is true that "the one who prays, saves himself and the one who does not, harms himself,"[11] it would be even more true that only the person who prays can reach sanctification. Isn't it toward sanctity that we have together launched our journey? Isn't this the main purpose of our conference call?

September 20, 1984

---

[11] *Cf. Alphonsus M. de Liguori,* Il Gran Mezzo della Preghiera, *Rome, 1984, p. 73.*

To Work with Perfection and with Love

During this month of October we are living the Word of Life: "Then give to Caesar what is Caesar's, but give to God what is God's" (Mt 22:21). Therefore, we should give to the State what belongs to the State.

We do not put this Word of Life into practice only by paying our taxes regularly to ensure the community of its various services, or by going to vote in political and administrative elections, but by carrying out our work for the community with an always greater sense of responsibility and commitment.

In this way we will all project ourselves into fulfilling the Holy Father's directive: "Grow and multiply." If last month we made the effort to grow in the love of God, which is verified through our life of prayer, in this month we will try to grow and to improve in the way we carry out our work. Work is—as we know—another aspect not only of our material life, but our spiritual life as well.

We'll try to improve our work, because through it—whatever kind of work it may be—we serve the community, and in this way we can give to Caesar what is Caesar's.

How can we improve our work and our various daily tasks? We must remember that behind those files that we speedily take care of, perhaps alone at the desk; behind the hard work to be carried out in the fields; behind the school lessons that we must prepare or the homework to correct; behind the machines that we must operate, the food we cook, the clothes we must manufacture, the talks or programs to be outlined, there are people, better, there is Jesus, who counts as done to Him all that we might do for the community or for individual persons, and it is still He who declares to us "Give to Ceasar what is Ceasar's."

If this is so, how should we perform our work? There is no doubt: with perfection and with love. We know that we must have a very high concept of the value of work. Therefore, it must be done with perfection.

Yet also—and this is what I would want to suggest today—it must be done with love.

With love. With love toward Jesus or towards those many Jesus' for whom we work.

Therefore we must keep in mind the presence of Jesus in each one of our neighbors, who perhaps await anxiously the process of material that bureaucracy seems so often to slow down; who await the bread which is produced after fields are harvested; who await the instructions to be received from our teaching, the clothes that serve their needs, the food to be nourished with, the inspiring word that keeps them alive and on fire in working for the Kingdom of God.

We'll try to accomplish all things so that they prove useful and appreciated.

We want to work, in other words, making ourselves one with the individual and with the collectivity we must serve.

To make ourselves one: an expression that always enlightens us. To make ourselves one: like God who out of love not only made Himself one with us, but also became a carpenter to serve others as a man Himself, to give to Caesar what is Caesar's.

To make ourselves one: to descend—if it is a question of doing so—to the level of our neighbors in need. To make ourselves one with their needs and wants, to be "them."

Charles de Foucauld, in speaking about the love which we owe to the others says, "... when we love someone, we are really in that person; we are in that person with love. We live in that person with love. We no longer live in ourselves, because we are no longer attached to ourselves; we are detached from ourselves, outside of ourselves. We no longer live in ourselves; we are in the one we love; we live of that person's life... As the Father lives in the Son out of love, and as the Son lives in the Father through the love He has for Him, we live in others through the love we have for them. And this is the way in which we must love all people."[12]

Let's in the next two weeks aim in this direction: let's do all things perfectly. The *Imitation of Christ* states, "the one who loves much, accomplishes much; the one who does one thing well, accomplishes much."[13]

May every work that leaves our hands be a masterpiece. But let's do it out of love: may our work be refined by the love that emanates from a heart which is guided by the voice of our conscience, enlightened by the Holy Spirit, who never holds back in admonishing us in the things we have not yet learned to do well, or in showing His approval by consoling us when everything is in order.

October 4, 1984

---

[12] *Charles de Foucauld,* Scritti Spirituali, VII, *Rome, 1975, p. 100.*
[13] *Anonymous,* Imitation of Christ, *Rome, 1984, p. 46.*

An Old, But New Commandment

Heartfelt greetings to everyone and an ardent wish for a marvelous Holy Journey.

I say this, because this is what is most important: to lead our daily lives in a holy manner, and to conclude our lives yet holier still, as certain brothers and sisters of ours whom God has called even just recently into the Next Life have done.

This has been true for Beppe Borla, and for Nick a wonderful married focolarino from the Philippines whom we must all remember and imitate.

In this month of October we are guided by the Word, "Then give to Caesar what is Caesar's, but give to God what is God's" (Mt 22:21).

If during the past two weeks we have attempted with great love to give to Caesar what is Caesar's, then during the second half of this month let's make the effort to give to God what is God's.

To give to God what is God's.

We have before us our friends of the Heavenly Mariapolis who warn us that life really does not last that long, and that our own passage to the Next Life may not be so far away. A desire surfaces to know what would be the best way to give to God what is God's.

It is the same question we first focolarine used to ask ourselves. Since war and death were always near, we wanted to know the best way to love God.

We all know the answer: it is to do the will of God, which asks us, extraordinary as it is, to practice the new Commandment of Jesus.

Last week, while I was at Instanbul, this same answer once again sprang forth from my heart in a powerful way.

Being in such direct contact with the heart of the Orthodox Church, whose spirituality someone defines as drawing deeply from the thought of St. John, I meditated each day on the first letter of this Evangelist.

As has happened on other occasions, I experienced its strong impact in seeing how much he emphasized the New Commandment speaking of it as if it were Jesus' Commandment, par excellance.

St. John defines this commandment as "old" and at the same time as "new" (cf. 1 Jn 2:7).

"Old" because as the letter says, we have it "since the beginning," from the moment we became Christians, and therefore, believers who have been baptized.

But also "old," a commentator explains, as Jesus Himself, the Word incarnate, who pronounced this commandment whose origins derive from divine life itself, and which are based on the very nature of God, who is Love.

It is "new" because, living it in such a sublime manner through His death on the cross, Jesus gave it life, enlightening and explaining it to the world.

Meditating on all these things, I realized once again, with immense gratitude, how well the Holy Spirit has guided us; among the thousands of roads we could have taken, He directed us to *the* road, to the heart of Christianity, to the commandment whose fulfillment is the purpose of all the other commandments.

The ardent desire I would want to share with you is to always try to live it better, trying to perfect it, aiming all our ascetic effort to live the Christian renunciation with which we must clothe ourselves, because loving in this way is not something merely natural, but supernatural.

Therefore, how can we give to God what is God's? By reconverting ourselves each moment to the New Commandment; not with words, but with deeds.

In this way we will be reassured of having done what was required, of having done everything.

October 18, 1984

Charity Means to Die, Not Just Being Ready to Die

Once again, we pick up our conference call to help each other gain speed on our Holy Journey.

The Word of Life of the month says; "Over all these virtues put on love, which binds the rest together and makes them perfect" (Col 3:14).

But what does St. Paul mean by the words "over all"?

In explaining Christian conduct, the apostle Paul often likes to use the image of the clothing with which the follower of Christ must be dressed. Do you remember? "... with truth as a belt around your waist, justice as your breastplate..." (Eph 6:14).

Also in the present passage which we are referring to, he uses the imagery of articles of clothing to speak of the virtues which must take hold in our hearts. They are: mercy, goodness, humility, patience, tolerance, forgiveness.

But "over all"—he says, thinking of a belt which binds everything together and gives the touch of perfection to wearing attire—"put on love."

Yes, love: because it is not enough for a Christian to be good, merciful, humble, meek, patient... Christians must show love toward their neighbors.

But someone might object saying, "Doesn't love mean being good, merciful, patient, and forgiving?"

No: Jesus taught us what love is. Love compels us to die for the others. Take note—to die. Not to be ready to die, but to actually die. To die spiritually, by denying ourselves in order to "live the others," or if it is the moment, to die physically.

Love, in fact, is not the readiness to give our life; it is giving our life.

Hatred takes our neighbor's life away ("anyone who hates his brother is a murderer," 1 Jn 3:15), love gives life to our neighbor. Christians have love, only if they always die to themselves for others.

But if a Christian has love—St. Paul says—this person will be perfect and each accompanying virtue will be brought to perfection: "Over all these virtues put on love, that binds the rest together and makes them perfect."

Surely, we too have acquired a certain habit of being well disposed toward our neighbors. We too are tolerant, and forgiving. But, if we observe ourselves carefully, what we are often lacking is really love. Even if we have the holiest of intentions, our human nature always draws us to look back upon ourselves, and consequently when we love the others, we do so half-heartedly.

We cannot be Christians if we are only living in this manner.

We must open our hearts to their widest extent. Before every neighbor that we meet during the day (at home, work and everywhere), we must tell ourselves: "Take courage, let's go, it's time to die." In this way, we live without thinking of ourselves, but thinking of others, living for others.

You know how (after having understood the New Commandment of Jesus in a new way) the Focolare considers as a milestone in its history, the pact that the first focolarine formulated: looking across to one another they said: "I am ready to die for you (meaning: I will die for you). I for you. Each one for the other."

Thereafter, it was as if that pact had become the very nature of the Focolare.

Therefore, we are all called to be living expressions of its fulfillment.

So then, in this month in which the Word of Life again invites us to be clothed in love, let's try, above all when we receive Holy Communion, to reformulate that pact: "With your help, Jesus, I will die to myself before every neighbor, beginning with those who share my ideal."

If we act in this way wholeheartedly, and try to be faithful to this pact in concrete ways, we will see the Christian revolution flourish all around us, and everywhere, with renewed vigor because—as we know—the Risen Lord will shine forth among us. We will then gather abundant fruits worthy of a God: conversion after conversion, vocation on top of vocation. In this way we will share the task in living out the Holy Father's directive: "Grow and multiply."

December 6, 1984

Charity is What Counts, Charity is What Remains

While reading the Statutes of the Focolare during these last few days, I experienced a new joy. I realized, in fact, how much God keeps us on track, because it is written that the general purpose of the Work of Mary is indeed charity, furthermore, the perfection of charity.

You know how spontaneously we often speak about charity, as if we have come to the awareness that in charity we find everything that God wants from us.

Now I am coming to the same conclusion (perhaps for the one thousandth time, but as if it were the first) that it is really charity that God demands from us: the norms that we have written down and which the Church has sealed as our way of life tell us this.

These norms keep us aware that we have been called, above all, to give to the world an exposition of perfect charity, that charity which is love for God and which is verified in the love of neighbor.

We also spoke about charity in the preceding conference call. We were all struck by the understanding that love for our neighbors does not mean to be ready to die for them, but to actually die, so as not to be ourselves, but to be the other, to live the others.

The impression it left seemed so strong and beneficial, that I was doubtful as to whether or not to propose a new thought for our journey. I was doubtful, but then I became convinced that it would be a good idea to hold on a little longer to this concept, to assimilate it better still, and to try and try again to put it into practice.

So, for this conference call, in order that our decision to die completely to ourselves before each neighbor may acquire greater commitment, I would like to examine again the importance of charity, this time with the help of two great saints who have successfully completed their Holy Journey: St. Augustine and St. Jerome.

Various ideas of theirs have left a deep impression on me, and so I hope they can do the same for you.

St. Augustine, a master of charity, makes this clarification: "If everyone were to make the sign of the cross, respond 'amen' and sing the alleluia; if everyone were to be baptized and were to flock to the churches; if everyone were to build walls for the basilicas, then all that would remain to distinguish the sons of God from the sons of Satan, would be charity.

Those who have charity are born of God, while those who do not possess charity are not born of God. This is the principal criteria for discernment. If you had all things, but lacked just this one, nothing you have would be useful to you; if you lack those other things, but you possess this one, you have fulfilled the law..."[14]

St. Jerome writes: "I ask you: do you know what it means to pass on from infancy to childhood, then to adolescence and to adulthood, then onto old age? We die a little bit each day. Each day we undergo a transformation, and in spite of this, we still live the illusion of being immortal. These very things that I am dictating, and that are put into print, which I then reread and correct, are all moments subtracted from the time remaining for me to live. Each mark that a printer leaves on the page, is a mark that is removed from a turning point in my life.... The only true profit that remains is our unity in the love of Christ."[15]

Have you understood?

What counts for us Christians is charity, as St. Augustine affirms; and as St. Jerome tells us, it is charity that remains.

What can we draw from this?

When during the day we may feel that our heart gives value to one detail or another, to the hope of leaving a good impression, to not lose face, to a sentiment, an attachment, to judgments, thoughts, feelings, persons, to ourselves, let's create the

---

[14]*St. Augustine, "Commento alla Prima Lettera di S. Giovanni," 5, 7, in:* Teologia dei Padri, III, *Rome, 1982, p. 250.*
[15]*St. Jerome,* Le Lettere, II, *Rome, 1964, p. 135.*

habit of putting everything aside, of eliminating all these things from our concern by repeating within ourselves: "This has no worth, nor does this thing," so as not to fill ourselves with vanity.

Instead, when we find an occasion to practice charity, let's reassure ourselves by saying: "This is what has true value, this is what counts, this is what will last."

In this way, we will live out our vocations as authentic Christians and as members of the Work of Mary. In this way we will put on that article of clothing that St. Paul speaks of in the Word of Life for this month: "Over all other virtues put on love, which binds the rest together and makes them perfect" (Col 3:14).

December 20, 1984

To Take the Initiative

The New Year opens with a splendid Word of Life: "But God is rich in mercy; because of his great love for us he brought us to life with Christ when we were dead in sin" (Eph 2:4,5).

The commentary to this Word of Life, which you may have already read, underlines two characteristics of the love of God. One is that God in His love took the initiative to love us even though we were anything but lovable ("dead in sin"). The second is that God's love did not reach only to the point of forgiving our sins, but since His love is infinite, He brought us to share in His very life ("he brought us to live in Christ").

These words and thoughts bring us back to the very beginnings of the Focolare, when God enkindled in our hearts the spark (the Pope would say) of our great ideal. In the light of this splendid Word of Life, I realize that spark or that fire was nothing less than our sharing in Love itself, who is God.

In the midst of the dreariness and desolation which surrounded us due to the war, was it we who found others taking the initiative to love us?

Through a special gift of God, weren't we the ones lighting the flame of love in many hearts around us, urged by the desire to see this flame ablaze in everyone? Did we choose to love those who appeared the most likeable or rather were we more attracted to the poorest of all in whom we could better recognize the countenance of Christ, and to sinners who most needed His mercy?

Yes, by a divine miracle, (the kind of miracle that occurs each time a charism of the Holy Spirit springs forth amidst the world), our own little hearts could attest to be rich in mercy.

As we know, loving our neighbors did not simply mean to make ourselves one with them to the point of bringing them to God. It meant to draw them into our revolution of love, our very ideal. We considered everyone to be a candidate to unity and therefore all could and did participate in that dynamic divine life that God had brought about at a given point in the Church's history. So it was at that time, and so it should be today. Certainly times have changed, but it shouldn't be difficult to admit that if the world at that time appeared to us as a desert because of the destruction of the war, the world today, even though the reasons may be different, shouldn't appear any less of a desert as well.

Many factors have contributed toward the leveling of our modern society; we live in a very ambiguous time.

At one time society at its basis was fundamentally Christian, and a clear distinction could be made between good and evil.

It is not so today. In the name of a freedom which is not true freedom, good and evil, observance and non-observance of the Commandments are all put on the same plane. We are living in a new kind of desert, where what has suffered bombardment are not homes, churches, and other buildings, but instead, moral law, and consequently, individual consciences.

What can be done about this?

Are we without arms in our battle to bring the forgiveness and love of Christ to a world which takes so little account of the reality of sin?

No, we are not without weapons.

This desecrated world has a countenance for us: Jesus Forsaken, in whom the sacred and the divine is completely hidden. In every negative situation, we see a reflection of Him; God who is abandoned by God. It is in His name and in our love for Him that we will find the strength to love what today appears so despicable. With the fire of love aflame in our hearts, and like our God who always takes the initiative, we will reach out to those we meet along our way. God, in us, will reawaken and enlighten consciences, instill contrition, bring back hope, enflame with enthusiasm, giving a desire to many, dead as they are, to be brought to life in Christ.

Therefore, the Word of Life in the month of January places before us three objectives: to keep the fire burning in our hearts; to be the first to love; to not measure our love, but to love boundlessly. In this way we will bring many to live our ideal, which is to live Christ.

Only if we live on this level can we be in line with what the Scriptures ask of us this month.

I'll conclude with the most ardent wish that you all have a most holy new year, rich in graces. It is the fourth year of our Holy Journey.

January 3, 1985

To Walk in the Way of Love with Love as Our Ever Present Companion

In our conference calls, we have spoken over and over again about love, and about love for our neighbors.

It is true; we are called to "the way of love." Pope John Paul II, in his visit to our Mariapolis Center, stated that love is the "core" of our spirituality.

It is also true that love of neighbor occupies such a place in Christianity that, having accomplished this, we have practically accomplished everything. Nothing we do has value unless it is accomplished in the exercise of love for neighbor. The saints have solemnly drilled this into our minds. We have become so convinced of this that our desire is to conduct our entire lives in this direction.

In order to walk in the "way of love," we can choose one of two methods. One is to make the resolution to love every neighbor that we meet, whether they be our neighbors with whom we work, live or for whom we pray. The other method is to love Love, who for us Christians is totally manifested and expressed in Jesus crucified and forsaken. To love, therefore, Jesus Forsaken. Experience has shown us that it is better to choose the second way. In fact, if I give my entire heart to Jesus Forsaken, He will always be there to give me suggestions on shaping my way of living, to prune my every action of all that is merely human; He will be there to invite me to embrace the fatigue that every task of mine requires, and to welcome every little or big suffering "always, immediately, and with joy,"[16] so that it will no longer be I who live, but the Risen Christ in me with His Spirit which is always alive.

---

[16] *A motto used within the Focolare which expresses the attitude to show in the face of suffering in order to be able to love always more.*

It is this Spirit, who is alive within me, who will give me the readiness to make myself one and to serve to perfection each neighbor I encounter; and not leave me in peace until I have fulfilled my task in doing so. It is a love which — as we have said in these past conference calls — makes me "die" for my neighbor. It is this Spirit, the Spirit of love, which gives me the greatest hope for my neighbor's spiritual growth and Christian fulfillment. This Spirit gives me the strength to love those who in some way are my enemy, because He suggests that I recognize His countenance also in them. He enriches my heart with mercy so as to know how to forgive and to understand my neighbors' troubles. He infuses me with the zeal to communicate to my neighbors in an opportune moment the most beautiful things in my soul, and to place them in the right disposition to walk more decisively on their Holy Journey.

Yes, I have seen and experienced that I walk better on the "way of love," having Love, Jesus Forsaken, as my ever present companion. The cross is the focal point of Christianity. Better still, Jesus crucified and risen is all of Christianity.

Let's go back then to placing Jesus Forsaken at the heart of our daily life as the guide to all our present moments to live. Let's go back to repeating: "I have only one Spouse on earth." We will come to the realization that we are walking swiftly on our Journey and living in depth the Word of Life that enlightens our month of January, teaching us to be, as God the Father, rich in mercy towards all.

January 17, 1985

Our Specific Road to Sanctity

Four years have gone by since we started our Holy Journey. Some of us have already completed this Journey, and have brought to Heaven as a special gift for Mary, the leader of our Work, the sanctity that they have reached.

Yes, four years. A desire comes from within to draw a balance on how our thrust to sanctity was lived. Taking a look behind us for just a moment (the only reason being so that we can walk better ahead) we see what characterized the beginning of our journey together. Knowing that to become saints we needed to live the virtues in a heroic fashion, and then encouraged by Sr. Gabriella *della Trappa* who reached the goal of sanctity[17] in such a short span of time, we made the commitment to live self-denial through the pruning and cutting involved in mortifying ourselves in order to eliminate our personal defects which we encountered along the way.

It was a period which — I am certain — brought us to experience many moments of joy, because of the life which flows forth from every pruning. The mortification of the "old man" places us continually on a supernatural plane, where joy and peace play a very precise role.

Since we had fought against our vices, it became a period in which we understood, in a more profound manner, the beauty of the various Christian virtues.

This period was followed by a second. Perhaps because we were guided by the Holy Spirit, we understood that although like all Christians we were called to self-denial, we could, better still, we needed to reach this goal, not so much by

---

[17] *Sr. Maria Gabriella* della Trappa *(beatified by Pope John Paul II on January 26, 1983) has been referred to at various times by the author as an example of someone who has run the course of sanctity very swiftly (cf. Chiara Lubich, Journey, cit., p. 19.)*

aiming at the death of our egos, but aiming instead at love, at love for others, "living the others." We discovered that we were already living the virtues through living love.

This path of love seemed much more simple and more in accord with our vocation, since the majority of us live in the midst of the world in continual contact with other people. In this period we also noticed many fruits and experienced deep spiritual consolations.

From time to time it appears to us, (the thoughts of the conference calls attest to this) that the Lord is bringing us to focus strongly on that principal aspect of our spirituality: Jesus Forsaken.

In fact, we have the impression that He insistently speaks within our souls words similar to these: "Are you looking for the way, your specific way to reach sanctity? It is I, Jesus Forsaken.

Do you want to find the model of self-denial, of the pruning that brings new life, of losses that produce gains, of the virtues with which you can clothe your soul, in particular, charity, the mother and queen of them all?

Do you want to find the model, the first to have walked the way of a collective sanctity, because on the cross, and more specifically through His apparent abandonment He took humankind along with Him, uniting all people to God and among themselves?

Look at me: Jesus Forsaken. He is your way, the complete way in which all your previous efforts and aspirations will find fulfillment."

Yes, Jesus Forsaken, who is the key to union with God; He is the way, *our* way to sanctity.

Therefore, as we have done so in the early days of the Focolare, let us also take this road today. At that time, nothing existed for us but Him; living our ideal meant above all to love suffering: our own personal sufferings, the sufferings of our neighbors, the suffering required in practicing the virtues and in spreading the Gospel. A revolution sprang forth, and the Focolare grew the way it did because we aimed our life in this direction. In fact, difficulties did not exist if out of love for Jesus Forsaken each obstacle became a springboard to go further ahead.

Today, let's go back solely to Him. Let's live our daily lives enriching the chalice offered by the priest at Mass with our small and big sufferings. Let's pour into that chalice many, even continuous acts of love for Jesus Forsaken.

Let's fill it to the point that the Lord can say: my chalice is overflowing.

This is our resolution.

We will see unprecedented progress in our personal and collective sanctity, and then abundant fruits throughout the life of the Focolare.

February 1, 1985

To Descend in order to Rise

The last time we spoke, we clearly understood that our road to sanctity has a name: Jesus Forsaken. He teaches us every secret along its path and is also the key for living to perfection the Word of Life for this month: "The fact is that whether you eat or drink — or whatever you do — you should do all for the glory of God" (1 Cor 10:31).

What does it mean to do everything for the glory of God? It means to act in a way that is pleasing to Him. We please God by observing His commandments, above all those regarding our neighbor. Therefore, this Word of Life could also be expressed in the following way: "The fact is whether you eat or drink — or whatever you do — do everything bearing your neighbor in mind, making yourselves one with your neighbor."

If we disregard the neighbor who is at our side, we cannot live for the glory of God.

To make ourselves one. The perfect model for making ourselves one is Jesus Forsaken. In fact, He made Himself completely one with us, except in sin. He who was of a divine condition, as St. Paul says (cf. Phil 2:7,8), lowered Himself to the point of taking on the condition of being a slave.

We want to become saints. But the true meaning of sanctity often escapes us. Sanctity is only love, because God, the Saint, is Love.

Many of us, since we are internal members of the Focolare, are often involved in the coordination of one or another branch, or of a zone, or of a focolare center, or of one or more nucleuses, a Gen unit or even a specific "work" of the Focolare. As we know, we often feel the zeal within us to perform our tasks to perfection, so as to give glory to God.

Yet, these positions of responsibility at times can be obstacles to sanctity. Because of them we may feel that it is a waste of time to share in our neighbors' smallest interests, but which for them are important; or to share in their toil and satisfaction in simple, hidden things.

Don't some fathers have this same attitude towards their child who wants to play a game or to go out to play sports? Can we not fall into this attitude toward those who do manual work, or toward those who need a certain distraction in order to rest, or toward those who spend their days in limited activity due to age or sickness? Examples are certainly not lacking.

Of course we should not fall short in our various commitments to the Focolare, yet we must know how to accomplish them in harmony with the love that allows us to make ourselves totally one with our neighbors, as Jesus Forsaken has done.

We will not become saints for having accomplished many things, but because we have loved much. Jesus in His abandonment does not appear to be accomplishing anything; He has no miracles to perform, nor discourses to give. He has only His body and His soul that can suffer for us and therefore, love us who are far from God. In that moment, He did not speak of love; He was Love who was concealing His divinity to share in our own poverty of being. It was there that He performed His greatest miracle, His greatest work: the salvation of all of humankind. It was there where He preached His most eloquent sermon.

We must remember that we have not been called to be perfect organizers, nor perfect leaders... We must be perfect in love. In this way, all these other perfections will be assured.

Therefore, the attitude which we must bear in mind, or the word which must not escape us during these next two weeks is this: *to descend* not because we, in some way, are on high, and the others lower, but because our ego, like a balloon, always tends to rise, and places itself in a position of superiority over the others, to want to make us feel in some way or another, "someone."

We must learn to be nothing, like Jesus Forsaken, who descended all the way to us, reaching as far as the greatest of sinners, and the poorest of all, both materially and spiritually.

This is the force that will help the others to ascend; it is like having the virtue of being a spiritual crane that can lift our neighbors out of the anguish of their sorrows, their worries, and their sufferings; from their personal complexes, their weaknesses or simply out of their own selves to go toward God and to reach out to their neighbors.

This is what is important: that we ourselves pass from death to resurrection, and that we help everyone else to do the same.

Let's remember: to descend, to know how to descend. We want to be spiritual cranes for the world around us.

February 21, 1985

To Walk with Jesus Forsaken

I hope you have all learned of the latest decisions we have made, which involve the recognition of Jesus Forsaken as being our only way; of the decision to walk side by side with Him. I am realizing more and more that He is our way.

Besides, in studying our Statutes, which is the task I must accomplish in this moment, I can see that this idea is already underlined. It is written that we must walk along the way of love, and we cannot arrive at unity without Jesus Forsaken.

Therefore, He really is the way.

If I can give an advice, the only one I would give is this; keep Jesus Forsaken always in mind, and try to accomplish all your resolutions through Him. For example, today you may say: "I want to live the will of God." Try to see the countenance of Jesus Forsaken in living the will of God, because without a doubt, in order to do the will of God and not our own will, we must deny ourselves, and in our self-denial, as we say, it is Jesus Forsaken who is present.

Another day you will say: "Today we must rest." In order to rest well, we must forget our apostolate, our work, our studies; we must, in some way, forget about everything. In order to live this "forgetting," we need to keep Jesus Forsaken in mind.

Let's try to discover the countenance of our Spouse everywhere, because we have only one spouse, not two or three. Let's keep this in mind for all the moments of our day, and for all the decisions that we need to make; in all the good ideas that come to us day to day to live our race toward sanctity, let's try to recognize Jesus Forsaken.

March 4, 1985

Keep On Playing

Luminosa[18] has so recently passed on from the earthly to the Heavenly Mariapolis, that I cannot but speak of her in this conference call.

I want to speak of her also because her life has so many beautiful things to tell us (and we are gathering many of them together) that it is not difficult to extract a few splendid pearls from the treasury of her wonderful soul. One of the lessons that this exceptional Focolarina leaves for us is how to live and conclude the Holy Journey, I would say, to perfection. I mention also "conclude" because she has taught all of us how a member of the Focolare should face death and live that moment in the spirit of our great ideal.

In September of '84, when hearing the opinion of her doctors that her sickness could run its course from one day to the next, I realized that I had to advice her that her life was drawing to a close. I told her the story of St. Louis, who in the midst of playing a game was asked the question, "What would you do if you had just found out that you were about to die?" He answered, "I would keep on playing."

Upon listening to my words, accustomed — as we say — to live in perfect unity with the person who represents the will of God, Luminosa fixed this phrase within her heart: "to keep on playing." She lived it to the letter, day after day, hour after hour, and had never allowed it to slip from her soul. Each time I went to visit her, she would ask me, as if to have a further confirmation, "I should keep on playing, shouldn't I?" And in the month of November when I was unable to visit

---

[18]*Margarita Luminosa Bavosi, a Focolarina from Argentina, died after a long sickness, on March 7, 1985. The name "Luminosa" was given to her by Chiara Lubich because of the great transparency of her soul.*

her as often because I was away from our headquarters, she would write to me: "I keep on playing."

For her, "to keep on playing" meant to live each day as a Focolarina, or even more, as a person who is aware of having a particular position of responsibility in the Work of Mary,[19] without expecting to prepare herself for death in any special way or method; it meant to spend all her efforts in keeping in touch with what is happening throughout the Focolare. She kept video equipment in her room, and she kept up to date on everything as if she were perfectly healthy. She received mail, she wrote, sent gifts and flowers, gave advise when asked, even on what regarded matters of the Work of Mary. She rejoiced in our joys, and suffered with us in our own sufferings. She lived her prayer life regularly. Naturally, she embraced her own physical sufferings, but in a way that no one would realize it. She lived in such a way as to make us think that she wasn't in much pain, while we knew that others, in her same condition, lament continuously. It wasn't so for her; her soul was so healthy that she appeared also healthy in body, even though it was becoming more difficult for her to breathe. She would affirm, "this is my life," and in loving this Jesus Forsaken perfectly, in a way that the Risen Lord shone forth from within her, she would "continue to play" and keep herself informed about everything. And this was the way she lived right until the end. We would want to say that she died "alive," she died perfectly healthy.

In her last few hours her attitude seemed to alter when — and here we see that practically nothing changed — realizing that she could no longer begin again because her breath was so short, she asked the Focolarine to make a pact as if to say; "I have finished (it was her *consummatum est*), now you must continue ahead." She continued "to play," and invited everyone else to do the same.

This is the lesson that Luminosa teaches us today. This is the motto of her marvelous spiritual ascent in this final portion of her Holy Journey.

---

[19]*For many years she was one of the national directors of the Focolare in Spain.*

This is the inheritance that she leaves us: the secret of knowing how to die as God wants, as Mary, our sweet Mother teaches her children: "to keep on playing," to continue to live our supernatural life without any worry for the future (even if it means our death), being completely attentive to the present moment in its joys and in its sufferings; in building the Work of Mary which is a Work of God; a Work we build here, and which we will find in Heaven, because our great act of love in doing so will be considered in our final examination.

What now? Let's follow Luminosa's proposal and adhere to her pact. She has finished her journey. Now it is up to us. Nothing can stop us from fully living our life as members of this Work, with the Risen Lord resplendent in our hearts. We will gather graces upon graces, as we have seen in Luminosa, and among these the grace to make a flight toward Heaven, toward that great encounter with Jesus and Mary.

Let's remember: even if we are warned that our death is drawing near, we must keep on "playing." Therefore, let's keep on "playing" in every other situation; as serious as it may be (from a human standpoint), it is always something less than death.

Let's keep on "playing," knowing that part of the game is to always begin again! It's a phrase that is pleasing to God and to Mary, who, when she reveals herself on this earth, asks for conversions. To always begin again is to be constantly converting. So then, let's keep on playing, let's keep on beginning again.

March 21, 1985

Building the Work of Mary
Through the Communion of Goods

In the last conference call, I said that our great act of love to bring to Heaven is *to build the Work of Mary*. Luminosa had done so, and concluded her life in a marvelous way; she kept on "playing," which means she kept on loving, building the Work of Mary.

And this is what we all must do.

In the work that we do, in our prayers that we raise to God, in the apostolate that we are engaged in, in the necessary care of our health, let's not see only a duty to fulfill, but, instead, let's see in them the many ceramic tiles that compose a mosaic; the many expressions of the act of love which Jesus will ask us to give an account of; let's see in them parts of the construction of that portion of the Work of Mary which we are responsible for.

Are we studying? Let's not do so only in view of an earthly exam, but to build the Work of Mary. Do we go out to meet others? To build the Work of Mary. Are we attending a sick person or helping a person who is near death to conclude his or her Holy Journey well? Let's do it to build the Work of Mary. Are we praying for our friends who have passed on from this life? Let's do so to build the Work of Mary. Are we praying to them so that they may also lend us a hand? Always for the Work of Mary. The Work of Mary, in fact, has greater horizons than the ones that we often give it through our own limited viewpoints. Like the Church, of which it is a small image, it is present on the earth, but also in purgatory and in the glory of Heaven.

This "building of the Work of Mary" was very clear to us in our early days, that period which remains as a fixed and luminous point for us.

We had understood that it could and that it must be said of us, as of Jesus, that "My food is doing the will of him who sent me and bringing his work to completion" (Jn 4:34).

This Word of Life produced a special resonance within our hearts. We understood, above all, that we shouldn't follow our own will; we must not have our own plans, but those of Another. It seemed to us that we could also say, in a certain sense, that we were sent to do the will of Another. Doing this will, also we would have been able to accomplish a work. And it was this continual effort to everyday search for His will that made it possible for us to build the Work of Mary step by step, which no one among us had foreseen.

Yes, we must *build the Work of Mary*. And if there is someone among us who does not know where to begin, or if there are others who wish to make themselves more available to this task, let's first of all lay its foundation.

We know what it is; what underlies everything; what must be the norm of norms. It is reciprocal love with all its consequences, as those indicated by the Word of Life for this month: "The community of believers were of one heart and one mind. None of them ever claimed anything as his own; rather everything was held in common" (Ac 4:32).

During the next two weeks, let's stop from time to time and take a look at all that is ours, whether it be of a spiritual or material nature, and let's think of it as something which is not ours, but belonging to the community, to the Work of Mary. It is given to us so that we can administer it well, and then place it at the disposition of the others.

Let's begin then, with this total detachment, ready to give up everything to Jesus in our neighbors. This is the basis for building the Work of Mary, for our *keeping on playing*.

Even though it may not seem so, we have many riches to put in common. We find them in our physical and intellectual powers. We have a tender heart to give, kindness to demonstrate, joy to share. We have time to place at the disposal of others; prayers, interior riches to put into common either by voice or in writing. At times we have articles, purses, pens, books, money, homes to place at the disposition of others, our cars etc.

For those who have what is necessary for their wardrobe, it can be a good norm, for example, according to one's vocation and apostolate, to put into common what is above one's needs, like clothing or other articles which arrive through God's Providence or which are even bought. We can try to do this without over-rationalizing, for instance in saying, "But this article can be useful to me on this or that occasion." We can always consider everything useful, but as we abide by these suggestions, our hearts become infiltrated with many attachments, and we create continual needs for ourselves. Instead, as each plant created by God absorbs from the earth only the water that it needs, let's also make the effort to possess only the things that we need. We are better off if once in a while we realize we are in need of something. It's better to be a bit poor, than a bit rich.

Certainly, if we live in this way, Jesus will not hold back in providing the hundredfold for us, which will give us a further possibility to give.

Then, to sum up, let's give to all of our actions the tone of *bringing to completion the Work* of God, which is our great act of love.

But so that all our actions may acquire their full worth, let's review our personal communion of goods.

April 4, 1985

To Die Rather Than not Love You Forsaken

We have just lived through this marvelous Genfest and the reactions of many young people throughout the world are arriving to our headquarters.

As you can imagine, they are very positive. However, what struck me most were the reactions of those who were encountering the life of the Focolare for the first time, whether they were believers, or more often, indifferent, agnostic, or non-believers.

The coldness in which the youth of our time live is striking. They seem to drift within a lifeless desert, without hope, warmth, ideals, without anything to live for. They live in discouragement and in a sense of resignation to it all. This sad condition of theirs places an ardent desire in our hearts to do something more so that the spark of an ideal may touch them and give them a breath of fresh air, open a way for them, and show them a future.

Today, I address these words to you and to all of us who are internal members of the Work of Mary, so as to increase our incentive to build this flame in our hearts higher and to set the blaze which, united, we can together maintain and spread.

What must we do so that this can occur?

We know that the will of God has indicated a road for us. It is a road that spells out sanctity, a fire of love for God and for neighbor; hope, therefore, for many around us. This road is Jesus Forsaken, chosen as our everything; preferred over every creature and thing; assurance of the full presence of the Risen Lord in and among us.

Without a doubt, on this past Good Friday, we have all consecrated ourselves to Him. But today, given the extreme necessity, I would ask of you, of all of us, a further step.

This choice must be radical: Him and no one else. To be

all His—without any compromising. *To be ready to die rather than not love Him forsaken.* To take this decision each morning and be faithful to it throughout the day.

Where can we find Him in order to love Him?

We know where: in all the small or big sufferings of our daily life; in the effort to make ourselves one with our neighbors; in knowing how to be patient; in suppressing each attachment to everything that is not the will of God for us in the present moment; in accomplishing everything with perfection—without hurrying, in perfect discipline, with intentions that are not merely human, but supernatural. We find Him in living our moments of prayer in a state of recollection; in overcoming our small and big personal vices; in preferring Him in those who most resemble Him; in taking the initiative to work for our goals that most remind us of Him: unity among Christians, with those of other faiths, with non-believers. We find Him in the effort it takes to keep this love alive in others so that the Risen Lord may be present among us. In short, in giving more value to victory over ourselves than to all the rest: in allowing Him, therefore, to emerge as the king of our existence.

Wherever in the Focolare this proposal and concern of mine have already reached, we have begun to live in this way. We have even adopted a method which was perhaps suggested to us by Our Lady (who is always merciful and concrete). We have decided to count these acts of love each day, knowing that this is what is of most value in our lives, and to offer them in the evening to Jesus.

Our experience thus far has been somewhat extraordinary. As never before, our souls have lived in true freedom: freedom from ourselves, from things, from everything. We have been overtaken by a wave of new joy: a joy, I believe, which is inherent to the Kingdom of God, which invades the hearts of those who are poor in spirit. We have noticed that living in this way, we can truly say that we can love God with all our heart, mind and strength, because we remove everthing that is not His will. Together with St. Paul, we can affirm that "All I know is Christ, and Him crucified" (cf. 1 Cor 2:2). We can state without any falsehood, "I have only one Spouse on earth." We can better understand the beatitude of those who—like Luminosa—being dead to themselves, die in the Lord: "Happy now the dead who die in the Lord!" (Rv 14:13). This makes us understand St. John of the Cross's invitation to fill our days with these acts of love.

Personally, I understood why St. Teresa of the Child Jesus said that the days in which she had most to offer were truly festive days.

Yes, this is what life is: "Whoever wishes to be my follower must deny his very self, take up his cross each day, and follow in my steps" (Lk 9:23).

Let's try it! Let's try to live in this way, counting our acts of love. Certainly, not for becoming proud of the numbers we reach, but to encourage ourselves to increase them. A new life will flourish within our souls, in our focolare centers, within our nucleuses, in our various Gen units.

Let's make the effort to never trade away this choice of Jesus Forsaken for any other—beautiful, good, and holy they may be. The very joys that Jesus gives us—let's offer them to Him. Besides, they are given to us so that we may have more courage to love Him forsaken.

In this way, we will live a continual Easter, and the Risen Lord will be resplendent within us. Because of the Spirit who will live in us, we will be like fountains that irrigate the desert of this world. We will see many people being given new life. The way is Jesus Forsaken. Wasn't the cross the means so that Jesus would rise again?

Therefore, let's hold on tightly to the Spouse of our soul.

We will soon discover Him to be the precious pearl for which it is worthwhile to sell all that we possess.

In the next two weeks, then, let's count our acts of love and offer them to Him.

April 18, 1985

How to be Another Mary

As you know, I am dedicating my efforts during this period of time toward laying out the first draft of the Statutes of the Work of Mary, to which we all belong. Having to give a description of its very nature, I explained what its characteristics are.

From one point of view, the Work of Mary reflects the Church: Pope John Paul II, during his visit to our Mariapolis Center affirmed that the features of the post-Conciliar Church can be recognized in the Work of Mary. From another viewpoint, our Work is a reflection of Mary, of whom it wants to be a continuation, a presence upon this earth, in both its entirety and in its singular members.

The month of May has just begun, a month dedicated to Mary. What comes to mind continually is this second characteristic, and I feel that there is no better way that we could honor the Mother of God than by living our specific vocation.

At one time, when we were young (I'm speaking of us adults), May was a month that we anxiously awaited. It was a month which brought a wave of joy, newness, and purity to our hearts. During all of its thirty-one days, we would honor Mary by bringing her flowers, decorating her altars, and even building little altars dedicated to her in our own homes. Besides these things, we didn't forget to offer her spiritual bouquets.

Today, as Foco[20] explains while narrating his own experience in a stupendous page of his diary, it is our soul that above all must be her altar, Mary's altar.

How can we do this?

---

[20] *The familiar name with which Igino Giordani was called by fellow members of the Focolare. He was a well-known Catholic writer, and the first married Focolarino. The text referred to can be found in: I. Giordani,* Diary of Fire, *New York, 1982, p. 73.*

How can we enthrone Mary? What must we do so that Mary, in a certain way, can take residence in our soul, as Grignion de Monfort explains?

Practically speaking, how can our lives be a continuation of Mary.

As we know, Mary is a monument of charity, and of all the other virtues. She reveals them in her desolation, and her litanies sing of them: she is most pure, most chaste, amiable, so attentive to the voice of the Holy Spirit to be called "Mother of Good Counsel"; she is most prudent, powerful, clement, faithful, "mirror of justice," "seat of Wisdom," "cause of joy" for all; so mortified in what is merely of this earth to be called a "spiritual vase"; so recollected as to be defined a "vase of renowned devotion"; she is strong as a "tower of ivory," and so on.

We must live in such a way that others can say something similar regarding our own lives.

How can we do this?

We know the answer: by loving Jesus Forsaken in such a way that the phrase "I would speak of nothing but Jesus Christ and him crucified" (1 Cor 2:2) may become a reality within us so that we may give glory only to Him: to Him in suffering, to Him in our detachments, in the effort required to live the virtues, in particular charity towards our neighbors, expecially towards our enemies, and towards those most similar to Him. With Him, we will be like Mary, strong, loving, pure, amiable, prudent, powerful, wise, clement, faithful, etc. But also like her we will be a "mystical rose," because from our buds, many petals will bloom. In fact, love for Jesus Forsaken, our Spouse, will make us mothers and fathers of many souls. Like her, we will be a "house of gold," *domus aurea,* because we will protect the presence, resplendent as gold, of the Risen Lord within us; we will be an "arc of alliance," because we will not break the pact made with Him to love Him above all else; "gate of Heaven" for many who will be saved through our love; "morning star" because we will shine like her amidst the darkness of this world; we will be the "health of the sick" because we will do all possible to relieve those who suffer; "refuge of sinners" because they will come to us when they wish to open their hearts; we will be "consoler of the afflicted" because we will bring joy to torn hearts, "help of Christians" for the dialogues which we will initiate.

Through our love for Jesus Forsaken, we can imitate Mary in many ways. I would even dare to say that those who have decided to love Jesus Forsaken appear already a bit like Mary, at least in some of these characteristics.

Wouldn't you call prudent a person who remains silent about something which should not be said? Strong, who loving Jesus Forsaken, is victorious in the battles of life? Pure, who for Jesus Forsaken casts temptations away? Aren't we consolers of the afflicted each time we bring a person in tears to smile, and refuge of sinners when through the love we have for Jesus Forsaken in them, they open their hearts to us?

Yes, through the grace of God, the image of Mary is already appearing in those who love Jesus Forsaken!

Therefore, we can only but go ahead during this month of May and continue to count our acts of love for Him forsaken, or better, to gather flowers and bring them to Mary so that she may offer them to Jesus. At the end of the month, we will find ourselves even more similar to her, and we will have brought the entire Work of Mary to correspond better to its marvelous vocation: to be a continuation of Mary in the world.

Our motto then should be: flowers for Jesus Forsaken in order to be another Mary.

May 2, 1985

How Mary Becomes Our Mother

We are still in the month of May and through this conference call I would want the love our hearts contain for Mary, the Mother and leader of the Focolare, to become even stronger.

In fact, oftentimes, especially by members of the Focolare who belong to other Churches (like the Lutheran, Anglican, or Reformed) I am asked to speak about Mary. Beneath this question, I can sense there is a desire to build a relationship with her.

In other instances, more often on the part of the Catholic members, I am asked what road could be taken or what method could be devised to increase a personal union with her; practically speaking, to be able to experience being her children.

Just in these past few days, while I was reading various writings on Mary, I realized how valid the experience of the Focolare is in this regard, and how our spirituality can uncover for many people the treasure of a filial unity with Mary.

The renowned theologian, Laurentin, in a chapter of his book *La Vergine Maria,* tells how, going back to the early centuries, the way to receive Mary from Jesus, as a Mother, in the way that St. John had received her, is already explained, for example by Origin, in the third century. The way he speaks of is living the Gospel.

Laurentin comments, "Those in fact, who understand and live [the Gospel] are identified with Christ and this identification permits them to be called, according to St. John 19, 26 'sons of Mary.'

Christians [who live the Gospel] with the help of grace, act in such a way that she becomes their Mother."

St. Nile of the fifth century is of the same thought. He

affirms that Mary is the "Mother of those who live in an evangelical way." Living the Gospel is, therefore, the way to have Mary as a Mother.

It is a great joy for us to know this, which gives us an explanation of the experience of the Focolare in this regard.

In fact, those who live the Ideal, which is nothing but the Gospel, experience at a given point of their life that Mary is their Mother; words spontaneously surface from within that express this relationship. This impression can be so strong as to be able to remember that first moment for the rest of one's life.

Another experience that can be made is to realize the difference between Mary, by now felt to be a Mother, and our own earthly mother. The love for our earthly mother, although it is great because it is refined and purified by supernatural charity, is still small compared to the love the Holy Spirit has placed in our hearts for Mary.

Thus, as the years pass, by persevering in living the Ideal, our relationship with our Heavenly Mother grows even though it may experience interruptions and setbacks.

This relationship grows. It continues to the point that after many years, one realizes that it has become more constant; that what before had veiled, in a certain way, our rapport with Mary (while our relationship with Jesus was more decisive) disappears, and Mary becomes totally present before our soul, and we can be in her company without any fear, as children with their own mother.

If we continue to walk the way of the Gospel, Mary, alongside of Jesus, will occupy a great place in our hearts as a door that leads to Him.

This love for Mary can become intense, very intense.

With Jesus and for Jesus, Mary becomes the love of our heart.

She is the aspiration of our soul, from whom after Jesus, our hearts can best rely on, the model that attracts us, yet which is beyond reach; she is the sweetness of our soul; the word that can best describe her—she is our "delight." This is truly so. The words that supernatural love draws from our hearts to declare to Jesus, can also be addressed to Her: I am all yours, Jesus, I am all yours, Mary, *totus tuus*.

Then, who knows what other experiences can be made in her regard by living the Gospel. We already realize however, that even the most difficult step to make, that of our own death, is sweetened by her presence awaiting us on the other side. She is the "trustworthy port of entrance."

Therefore, if this is so, if already in the early centuries it could be seen that living an evangelical life is the way to discover Mary as a Mother, we cannot but walk ahead guided by the Word of Life.

In this latter half of May, we will continue to gather flowers: they are the expression of our self-denial and of our love and embrace of the cross. This is the Gospel.

We deny ourselves above all when we love our neighbors and when we embrace the crosses that this love requires. Besides, these are the crosses that we are especially called to nail ourselves upon: the crosses that are inherent to the New Commandment.

During the following days, let's focus our attention above all on these crosses. They offer us the possibility to create a special bond with Mary because the New Commandment is the Gospel, in fact, the very core of the Gospel. And when our hearts possess this unity with Mary, life truly becomes something of another nature.

Flowers, therefore, for Mary, gathered through living reciprocal love.

May 16, 1985

Through Self-Denial We Allow the Holy Spirit to Act More Freely

In these past few days, because the contact with our Buddhist brothers and sisters is always so alive, I am studying their teachings more in depth. I am coming to the realization of how, by having strongly underlined a particular attitude—which is also at the basis of authentic Christian life—which is self-denial, this religion has so widely spread throughout the world that it has become the fourth largest, after Christianity, Islam, and Hinduism.

Buddhism, in fact, in the desire to free people from suffering, through its so-called "eight-fold way," practically speaking, asks for three things: morality (through the refusal of falsehood, of useless talk, of spreading scandal and through the abolition of adultery, of theft and murder); spiritual discipline, for example, blocking out evil emotions in favor of good ones; and finally the "proper knowledge" of things and the "right attitude."

Basically, we could say, it demands that we bring the "old man" in us to die.

And so, while reading this, I wondered what the Christian world would be like, and what would be the further developments in our own religion if all of its principles were lived in their fullness. But, in the meantime, let's focus now on self-denial, the typical Christian denial which is implicit in our love for God and for neighbor.

Of course we would not expect only to experience a certain freedom from suffering (in a Christian manner, naturally, through a particular alchemy that transforms, through the cross that is loved, suffering into love), but we will also be spectators of a continual, authentic Pentecost in many souls, of an invasion of the Holy Spirit in many hearts and minds.

This is what this month's Word of Life makes us aware of. It speaks about what a Christian is, and what distinguishes

Christians from others. Christians are sons and daughters of God because they are guided by the Spirit of God.

The Word of Life says, "All who are led by the Spirit of God are sons of God" (Rom 8:14).

But, in order that the Holy Spirit may act in us, our own response is needed. In writing this Word of Life, St. Paul was thinking above all about the Christian duty to practice self-denial, the struggle against egoism in its most varied forms, the death of the "old man." As for the rest, we know what to do: love for Jesus Forsaken, which means the effort to be exercised in living the virtues even to a heroic measure, calls for room within us for the Holy Spirit to act more freely. There is a link between the cross and the Holy Spirit, as the one between cause and effect. We experience this everyday: every cut, every pruning, every "no" to our ego is a source of new life, of peace, of joy, of love, of interior freedom; an open door for the Holy Spirit.

Therefore, here is our commitment for the next two weeks. We have finished with counting our acts of love, but not with accomplishing them.

Now that we have acquired somewhat a habit of doing so, let's accelerate our pace: no, no, no to our ego, and yes, yes, yes to God.

We will allow the Holy Spirit, who lives in our hearts, to work more freely. He will be able to lavish upon us more abundantly His gifts; He will be able to guide us; we will be recognized as being children of God.

Let's aim at denying ourselves this time, only for love of Him, whose feast has just recently been celebrated.

Besides, the undertaking that we have begun through this Holy Journey, that of building our sanctity, depends on Him. The Holy Spirit is the sanctifying God.

We must become His friends.

Therefore, once again: let's live self-denial better, so that our hearts might better contain Him.

Even more, in order to love and honor Him better, let's make Him the subject of our meditation. The Scriptures speak of Him (let's not forget the Acts of the Apostles), as do the books of meditation that we have.

But there are also other books and pamphlets that are very

beautiful. Let's memorize some prayers dedicated to the Holy Spirit—such as the *Veni Creator Spiritus,* if we don't already know it, so that we can recite it in our hearts. To sum up, let's do everything possible so as to know, love and pray better to Him.

The Holy Journey for all of us (more than fifty-thousand people) will acquire a new degree of quality. Then the truth, which is our faith, will be more known, the Kingdom of God will reach further ground, and the Holy Spirit will renew many things.

June 6, 1985

To Be Charged with Love

As I have often done before, also this time I would like to speak to you about charity. We are in the month of June, and the Word of Life speaks to us about the Holy Spirit: "All who are led by the Spirit of God are sons of God" (Rom 8:14).

As we know, the Holy Spirit infuses charity into our souls.

Therefore, if we have love for the Holy Spirit (which is what we hoped to intensify through our last conference call), we must keep in mind the gift that He gives, if for no other reason than to express our gratitude.

Charity is a topic, a reality of Christian life that forever astonishes me. Perhaps it is because the measure in which we must live charity is so great that it surpasses any effort we make.

This is the way I felt during these past few days after coming across the words: "In this way you will be truly sons of your Heavenly Father who makes the sun rise on the bad and the good alike, and causes the rain to fall on those who do the will of God and those who don't" (cf. Mt 5:45, Lk 6:35). I asked myself: do I really love the good and the bad with the same measure? Do I act in the same way whether with one or with the other? Do I pray with at least the same intensity and with the same love for those who love God, and therefore who love me, as for those who are distant from God and His commandments?

I saw that there is always something to improve on and to perfect. With this in mind, I experienced a new understanding of the following words: "Owe no debt to anyone except the debt that binds us to love one another. He who loves his neighbor has fulfilled the law. The commandments, 'You shall not commit adultery; you shall not murder; you shall not steal; you shall not covet,' and any other commandment there may be are all summed up in this, 'You shall love your neighbor as yourself.' Love never does any wrong to the neighbor, hence love is the fulfillment of the law" (Rom 13:8-10). I understood once again how great the beginning of our adventure was: the choice of God-Love; to love Him, and to do so by doing His will which is to love, to love one another... It came to me as somewhat of a rediscovery, a refocusing on what Christianity is. And I understood better, why, in our early years when we used to travel throughout the cities of Italy announcing our Ideal, the comment often made by bishops and priests, who knew our religion more in depth than we did, would be "It is Christianity! It is simply Christianity!"

Yes, we must be grateful to the Holy Spirit, because with the gift of the Ideal, he had offered to us no more, but no less than a new understanding of our religion, which is basically nothing but Love.

I encouraged you last time to say: No, no, no to our ego, and: Yes, yes, yes to God. How can we say our yes to God? We do so by inserting ourselves into the dynamism of the very life of God, which is Love. Our Christian faith, in fact, is faith in God who is Love, but not just a mere knowledge or an adherence to this truth. Our faith involves the participation of our very selves in the Love of God. The phrase "we have believed in Love," which characterized the life of the first Focolarine and which must characterize our life now, is not only a question of faith, but also of charity. If we believe that God is Love we must love, we must love one another.

Therefore, we cannot conceive to be Christian without this dynamism, without our hearts being charged with love. If a watch is not charged, it cannot function or give the time — we can say that it isn't a watch, but only a mechanism made of metal.

In the same way, a Christian who is not always aiming to be in an attitude of love, is not a person who merits to be called Christian.

To draw a conclusion: Let's take a look at ourselves during the day: are we showing our love for God, and therefore for His will and for our neighbors? Are we, so to speak "charged"? Do we have the charge of Christian love?

If this is so, everything will go well. In the evening we will not have to look back and list our errors. Those who love do no wrong. We will realize that we have always loved Jesus Forsaken, because with love we will have gone beyond each of our sufferings. We will discover that we are going against the current of the world because we will have thought only of God and of our neighbors, while those who love the world seek to satisfy their ego. We will come to the realization that Christianity is a totally positive, fascinating religion, which we could not but have followed; we will continue to share in all the extraordinary consequences that the Gospel, when lived, promises.

Yes, we must love! Let's go back to the beginning of our adventure. If we live it, our lives become complete, everything brings fullness.

June 20, 1985

Pray like Angels, Work like Laborers

In so many different places, the month of July has been very rich in apostolic activities including magnificent Mariapolises and congresses.

Before leaving Rome, being together during the Coordinating Council with those who hold various responsibilities at the headquarters of the Work of Mary, we made the intention to deepen our prayer life during these past few months.

For this reason, during meditation I looked again to the saints and to the experts in this field to see how our prayer life, which we already live, can be guided and to find new incentives to improve it.

As you already know, there is a distinction to be made in this regard: the first way of praying is what is called "vocal prayer," which consists in speaking with God utilizing prayers already established. A second and more perfect form of prayer is what is improperly called "mental prayer." This prayer consists in a spontaneous, loving and frequent dialogue with God and therefore—as St. Teresa of Avila, gifted with a special charism in the order of prayer, explains—"not in doing much thinking, but in loving much."

Now, for those who walk towards God in a way that is for the most part an individual one, "mental prayer" is a conquest that could require time, and at times a conquest that could be very difficult and not always reached.

Instead, for those who walk on a more collective way as our own (where the Holy Journey of life is made together with others, furthermore, where our neighbor becomes our way to reach God), I think that we can affirm that "mental prayer" (this loving dialogue with God) is not only common, but is practiced, at least in certain moments, right from the beginning.

Our experience, in fact, is that after having loved Jesus in our neighbor during the course of the day, when evening comes we find a deeper rapport with God. We discover His love for us and a confidential dialogue with Him begins to open within our hearts, which in time, and with the passing years can be the foundation of every action we make, and underlie everything we do.

I think that this is an experience we all make, and that it is an immense grace which we need to protect so as not to lose its strength.

What keeps alive this manner of praying ("mental prayer," this living dialogue with God), for us and for those who walk other spiritual paths, is the faithful adherence to the moments of prayer that God asks of each one of us (morning and evening prayer, attendence at Mass, meditation, etc.).

These prayers should be said very well. The experts say that for this to be so, we need a general and a specific preparation.

The general preparation would be to maintain our hearts free from any attachments.

It seems to me that all of us are committed to this kind of preparation. Isn't our entire life focused on loving Jesus Forsaken? Don't we always speak of detachments, of prunings, and above all of the detachment required in being projected outwards in our love toward the others, in living the 'others' and not ourselves?

Yes, this preparation is present in our lives. To say the least, it is what we daily strive for.

But, we need a specific preparation: to choose above all the most suitable environment for each of us to pray well. This could be our rooms, a church, a garden, a spot in the midst of nature, etc. We need to recollect ourselves in silence and since our soul is so bound to our bodies, we need to find the proper position to pray (whether on our knees or seated, with our hands folded or placed in another reverent position).

It is a necessary preparation that perhaps we must improve on. This allows us: to better carry out the will of God to pray; to not waste our "vocal prayer" through which we tell Jesus many stupendous things; to keep our dialogue with God alive in our hearts during the rest of the day.

In Heaven, where we hope to go, life will not consist of carrying out an apostolate, as it will consist of praising, thanking and adoring God, the Most Holy Trinity. We must learn now how we will live then.

Right from the beginning we realized the need for prayer. We were all familiar with and lived this motto: "Pray like angels, work like laborers." Along with others, this motto served to help us carry our Ideal ahead, and to spread our revolution.

The Focolare is an earthly and heavenly undertaking. It serves principally to extend the bounds of the Church. Jesus Himself, who founded this stupendous Spouse, would once in a while withdraw to the mountains to be in contact with nature in order to pray, and there He would speak to the Father.

Today, without a doubt, we live the second part of this early motto of ours: "work as laborers." We know that throughout the Focolare we have many commitments, and it is not rare that some of us become exhausted from over-work.

Is this balanced out by the first part of the motto? Do we pray like angels?

If this is not so, do we want to be so ungrateful towards God who opened us so easily to a communion with Him, and who gave us the gift of this so-named "mental prayer," that we do not want to do everything possible to maintain, deepen and render this prayer more frequent?

During the next two weeks then, let's keep in mind the thoughts that I have mentioned. At the end, we will find that we have spiritually progressed. And this is what we must do, because those who do not go ahead, go backwards.

August 1, 1985

"I Feel Very Happy"

We have just celebrated the feast of Saint Clare, as it is traditional to do throughout our "ideal world."[21] Your telegrams, messages, telephone calls and various gifts were all well appreciated. I want to thank you for all these things because it is, above all, the participation of all which makes us feel as if the entire Focolare palpitates as though it were one single heart.

And now we are once again linked together for our bi-weekly appointment. As you know, the reason for transmitting this spiritual thought is to help us to travel this next stretch of our life's Holy Journey in the best way possible. But who can better instruct us on how to travel this road of our existence than someone who has already splendidly completed its course?

For this reason, I would like to speak to you this time about Margrit, our married Focolarina for whom we are praying throughout the world.

You know how Luminosa will always remain for us as the person who has taught us to prepare ourselves to die, or better still, to always live "keeping on playing." Margrit instead will always remain in our minds as the one who has "reconciled us with death."

Death as we know, is a serious matter that holds both fear and mystery.

We can speak often about this dark passage to the next life, we can spend the whole of our lives preparing for it, but moments will never lack in which we can become fearful of it. Death, in fact, does not coincide well with the life we live

---

[21] *The geographical areas in which the Focolare lives out its spirituality of unity, called also the "Ideal," meaning God as our ideal.*

because it is a harsh and inevitable consequence of sin. With her death, Margrit has left us with an ineffable gift: she caused our hearts to cry out, "If this is death, then let's welcome its arrival!"

To die is a marvelous reality!

In short, she has completely reconciled us with death. I was close to Margrit during all of last year, when her soul passed through such difficult spiritual trials that they couldn't but make us think of the "dark nights" of the saints. Those who were aware of this, had they not known Jesus Forsaken, would perhaps have remarked, "But, this is too much!"

I went to visit her for the last time a few days before she expired. She was there lying in bed, reduced to just skin and bones, but with eyes that were so beautiful and alive which would open and then close, entering into a sleep that preluded her death. After I assured her that I would keep the presence of Jesus in the midst with her, I asked her, "Margrit, are you happy?" She responded, "I'm very happy, very, very happy!" Then, opening and closing her eyes she added, "I don't have any worries. I'm very happy, very, very happy."

Having seen such fullness in her heart I said to her, "You are going to Jesus and Mary. Would you greet them also in the name of the entire Work of Mary?" She answered, "Of course, of course." Then I asked, "Would you also greet Foco for me and all the others in the Heavenly Mariapolis?" And knowing how much she was purified by God I added, "Just think, Margrit, you will be in Heaven and there will be such a festive atmosphere." And she answered, "Yes, it seems incredible!" as if to say "It's something superlative, it's too beautiful!"

Then looking at me as she smiled so splendidly, which brought to mind the last unforgettable smiles on the face of Foco, she said, "I am like Jesus." I replied, "Like Jesus Forsaken" seeing in her dying a reflection of Him. "Yes," she said, "but I'm very happy."

I realized that I was witnessing an extraordinary phenomenon with my own eyes: the phenomenon of the Risen Lord which irradiates fullness of life in a body that is reduced to nothing, the phenomenon of the grace of God which bursts forth with all its power. In fact, while Margrit's human life, like a candle's flame, was dying out, another vibrant flame was enkindled within her, another Life, powerful, brilliant and so loving: that of Life eternal. Yes, I can attest to having contemplated the existence of eternal Life.

From a human point of view it was a phenonemon that was absolutely beyond explanation.

I kept saying to myself, "The saints must have died in this way!" If I or we would be given the possibility to die in the same way! Death in this case is a stupendous occurrence.

I spoke to her relatives and found them all serene, enveloped as they were in an atmosphere of such grace. Then, when I went back to see her and to give her a kiss, I told her, "Margrit, the Risen Lord lives within you." And I think that this was the most beautiful assurance that I could have given to a Focolarina.

Margrit, therefore, has fully reconciled us with death.

Dying can become an occasion of inexpressible joy.

Let's live in such a way as to also arrive ourselves at that moment in the same disposition as Margit's, and to merit the same graces.

But tomorrow we will be able to reconcile ourselves with death, if today we reconcile ourselves with life, with its problems and pains, with our efforts to live the virtues that life requires of us, and with our thrust toward always embracing what is most difficult. In short: our preference for Jesus Forsaken.

May Margrit help us redirect our journey, which we must always do, towards the death of our ego so that the Risen Christ may live in us from this moment on.

If our consciences today can assure us that the Risen Lord lives within us in each passing moment, then tomorrow, in that final moment, there will be someone who will confirm that to us, and for us there will be no death: we will pass on from life to Life.

So then, during these next two weeks, let's embrace Jesus Forsaken so well that the Risen Lord be always resplendent in us, yes, to the point of being able to say in each moment as Margrit did, "I am very happy. Very, very happy."

August 15, 1985

Being a Gift of Ourselves in order to Be

The Word of Life which enlightens this month of September is: "Whoever wants to be first, must make himself last and be the servant of all" (Mk 9:35).

This is a Word of Life that is very significant for us. Who among us, in fact, has never desired in various moments in life to be the one today who loves Jesus the most, and therefore to be the first? Who has not, urged by a strong invitation of the Holy Spirit, specifically asked Him, "Grant me the grace to love You in a way that no one has ever loved You"?

So then, if we want to reach this goal, we need to put ourselves in the last place and be of service to everyone. As the commentary to the Word of Life explains, this simply means to be in an attitude of love before each person we encounter.

Love, therefore is the way to reach the first place. This is what the Gospel teaches to all Christians.

However, for us love means more specifically to be members of the Focolare. As members of the Focolare our initial choice is God who is Love.

I have read splendid thoughts during these past few days on the Love of God. They had a very positive effect on my soul, and therefore I would like to communicate them to you. They are truths that we know very well, but it is good to hear them again, especially by those who are not familiar with our Ideal. "God is Love and therefore He communicates Himself.... He is a total gift of Himself. This communication of Himself is His nature, and therefore a vital law of His being. He does not exist but in giving of Himself, and this gift is His life. The divine being is therefore one, but He is not alone. Divine life is and must be a society of persons."[22]

---

[22]*Cf.* Diz. encicl. di spiritualità, I, *Rome, 1975, p. 303.*

God, therefore, is one, but He is not alone. In fact He is a Trinity of persons.

These considerations made me think of the way we live in the Work of Mary, and I saw in them a reflection of the Ideal we have chosen: God, who is Love. Also for us, Love is our life. Also in the Work of Mary, because we love, we do not remain alone, because love generates communion.

Only in this way are we Christians and members of the Focolare.

Love gives us our being. We do not exist only because of love; we exist because we love. If we do not love — and in all the moments in which we do not love, we no longer are — we do not exist. We neither live as Christians nor as members of the Focolare.

Therefore we must be love, and live this reality at the heart of the Work of Mary, as God lives it in Himself and is Love. In our focolare centers, our nucleuses, in our Gen units, our *grappoli,* in every structured component and in all of the Work of Mary, between the different branches and movements, God asks of us only this: to be a gift of ourselves to the others. St. Paul would say that it is the only debt that we have (cf. Rom 13:8).

But since God is Love not only within Himself, but outside of Himself, (in fact He has loved us and has sent His Son for us,) we must be a gift of ourselves for those who are outside of the Work of Mary, and even outside of the Church, who either do not belong to the Church, or have separated themselves through indifference, centuries-long divisions, or religious and cultural differences. We must take care of them. We can do this well by giving of ourselves, putting ourselves in the last place, which means to love them. Also here then, we will not be alone. The gift of ourselves calls for a gift as a response and many hearts will be turned to God.

"Woe to he who is alone," the Scriptures say (cf. Ec. 4:10). We must not understand these words to mean only that the person who is alone is in danger, but that he who is alone is so, because he does not love; he has not made a gift of himself. Woe then, to the person who does not love.

During these next two weeks we should examine our situation within the Work of Mary, which then means our situation within the Church.

We have to bear in mind just one objective: to be a gift of ourselves in every moment.

If we are a gift of ourselves to those who share in our Ideal, then the unity of the Work of Mary will grow, which we must never take for granted, but continually build.

If we are a gift of ourselves to those who are in any way far from God (persons, and relatives to be recontacted, non-believers, persons who ignore our Ideal, which if it is a charism, is made for everyone), then we will draw closer to *ut omnes* (that all may be one).

Let's then continuously ask ourselves, "Am I a gift of myself in this very moment?"

September 5, 1985

"Fully Present"

If there are two concepts that often reappear in our conference calls, they are sanctity and love.

In fact, like mountain climbers joined by a rope, we are all united to transform our life into a Holy Journey and we believe that the best way to accomplish this is by loving.

But is it truly by loving that we will become saints?

As we know, Christians are already made holy through baptism because the one who is the Saint—God, the Most Holy Trinity—lives in their hearts. St. Paul called the Christians of his time "saints" (cf. Col 3:12; Ep 5:3).

But more than anything else, by sanctity we mean something different: perfection. Saints are those who have corresponded perfectly to the gift of baptism.

Now, is it actually by loving that we will reach perfection?

In the history of the Church, has it always been by loving that Christians have become saints?

If we take a deeper look, we see that even though sanctity has always been proposed by the Church as the highest expression of love, it has not always throughout the centuries been presented in a clear fashion.[23]

In the first few centuries, for example, the saints, par excellence, were the martyrs. Then, martyrs became rare (due to the cease of persecutions), and those considered saints were the monks, whom the lay people would try to imitate in order to become good Christians.

We know how learned Foco was in regards to the period of the Fathers of the Church. He would often refer to an idea of St. John Chrysostom, that a married person had to live as a monk, except for celibacy. At that time monks and laypersons

---

[23]Cf. ibid., II, pp. 1661-1670.

did not perceive sanctity as a way of love, but as an escape from the world and as the practice of the evangelical counsels. Therefore the underlying tone of their spirituality was predominantly a negative one.

This attitude continued on into the Middle Ages. Even though St. Thomas Aquinas, according to the doctrines of the early Church—emphasized particularly by St. Augustine—had clearly reaffirmed that Christian sanctity is achieved through love, (and therefore can be reached in every situation and state of life, since it lies, above all, in living the commandments, and only secondarily by virtue of the evangelical counsels). All the same, the Christian world did not show much progress in this direction, preferring to keep an excessively ascetic and monastic attitude.

However, at the end of the Middle Ages, through new situations created by the Renaissance period, fleeing the world and physical penances were less emphasized, and greater consideration was given to interior self denial.

It was St. Francis de Sales who reintroduced the concept of love as the basis of Christian piety, and who brought into relief once again the possibility of reaching sanctity in the midst of the world.

So then, little by little, love as a means to sanctity was making its way ahead.

This is so also today, even though—as we know—the horizontal aspect of charity is often overstressed. In any case, love is the principal agent of sanctity. The Second Vatican Council also states this (cf. LG, chapt. 5).

It is love.

And we who, without the influence of others, have had the fortune of being guided directly by the Holy Spirit on the way of sanctity through a special charism of His, see how suitable to our times is this road that God has opened up, and how modern He is.

This realization must give us new vigor to travel such a road with the fullness of hope and joy.

There is no doubt that it is by loving that we can reach sanctity.

We also saw in our last conference call, how in order to live the Word of Life which invites us to take the last place in order to gain the first, we must love, we must be a gift of ourselves.

What shall we do then in these next two weeks? *We must perfect ourselves in love,* in love for God and for our neighbor. We will make the effort to be an even more perfect gift of ourselves still, for God, meaning for His will and particularly for that will of His which we find in loving our neighbor.

We must allow the charity that the Holy Spirit has infused in us to penetrate every fiber of our being. This charity must become incarnate in us, in our hearts and in our affections. It must assume our entire being: heart, mind, memory, will, and strength. During the course of our day, we must be *fully present* in the will of God of the present moment. "Fully present," without holding onto anything, anything, anything for ourselves, because what we hold onto we lose, and what we lose out of love, we gain. "Fully present" is our watch-word for the next two weeks: "Fully present" in the fullest recollection while we pray. "Fully present" in sharing our neighbors worries, interests, sorrows, doubts, and even joys. "Fully present" in embracing Jesus crucified and forsaken in our sufferings, sicknesses, and if it is the case, in death. "Fully present" in our study and in our work. "Fully present" when we need to take care of something that may seem to have only secondary importance, but that is always an important aspect of love, as keeping things in order, relaxation and rest. "Fully present" in the necessary detachments which the virtues require. "Fully present" to love, to be love, to place ourselves among the last, which means among the first in following Jesus.

September 19, 1985

To Improve

As you know, the important news that I want to inform you about today concerns the recent audience with Pope John Paul II. I was invited to have lunch with him because he wanted to celebrate — in his words — the anniversary of his visit to the Mariapolis Center on the 19th of August last year. During that blessed occasion, in that hour and a half in which we spoke of many things, I also addressed a question to him, "Are you satisfied with the Focolare?" He answered, "Yes, yes. Thank God that it exists! When I visit another country or city, and find that the Focolarini are there, I feel more...at peace, especially with the young people."

He affirmed that there is a charism in the Focolare, and that if St. Paul would today list the charisms that are present in the Church, he would say: Focolarini, etc.

The Holy Father sees, therefore, that there is a charism of God in the Focolare.

And therefore it is a grace to be a part of it.

It is a grace, it is a special talent of which we must be aware of in order to correspond to it.

This is the point that I would like us to focus our attention upon today: we must correspond.

I know that we are living our Ideal. I know that for many of you the Ideal is everything. How then can we be sure that we are doing all our part to make use of such a grace?

A method or system which is very useful to me, and which keeps me in the thrust towards sanctity, is the constant thought, renewed each day, that I cannot be satisfied to live as I did yesterday, but I must improve.

Spiritual directors, among other things, give this idea to be put into practice: to make the resolution to improve always. They know, as we know also, that in the spiritual life, those who don't go ahead go backwards. Therefore, it is an obligation to improve. To improve in what way? To improve in the love of God and neighbor, in embracing Jesus Forsaken in the sufferings and efforts required in living the virtues, to improve in living the Word of Life, etc.

For these next two weeks I would make the proposal to concentrate our efforts on improving an aspect of the will of God for us which is prayer. The Word of Life this month suggests it: "To God, everything is possible." Therefore, given that many things are possible only to God, we need to pray.

In living a spiritual life, we must rely greatly on the help of God, much more than we generally do. It is God who accomplishes the most important part. So as not to risk failure by trusting solely on our own efforts, we must pray to God so that He might send us His grace.

And how can we improve our prayer? Let's pause for a moment of silence before our morning or evening prayer, or before saying the rosary, so that we can be aware of whose presence is before us, and then assume the proper spiritual attitude and the most respectful bodily position.

If it is possible, let's pray before an image that helps us in our recollection and in our devotion. Let's pronounce our prayers slowly, without feeling rushed, in a way that they become our own words in which we place all of our hearts. We will soon realize that a prayer said slowly and well is light, and is not a cause for boredom since in the present moment it unites the soul with its God; while a prayer said hurriedly and clumsily weighs the heart down. Each time, then, that we get distracted, we must reestablish our union with God, with Jesus, Mary and the saints.

When we have completed our prayers, let's wait yet a few seconds longer before leaving our divine Guest. Let's not speak about other things while in church, or if we need to, let's do it in a whisper.

But oftentimes, we are engaged in spontaneous prayer as in our meditation, or during mass, or in the visit to the Most Blessed Sacrament. Even in these cases, let's choose to spend a few moments in silence, not only to place ourselves in the best condition for such a conversation, but also to be able to listen within to what may be the response of the Most Holy

Trinity who lives within us, of Jesus or of Mary.

Then let's speak and confide to God, to Jesus, to Mary, our most secret thoughts; let's tell them how much we love them, or would want to love them; how much we need them; what our difficulties are, our hopes, our projects. Let's always ask for the Holy Spirit. In short, let's get accustomed to an open dialogue with the inhabitants of Heaven.

If in certain moments this is not possible, because we may find ourselves seized by explainable or inexplainable darknesses, there will always be the possibility to speak to Jesus Forsaken and to embrace Him in these spiritual sufferings. The important thing is not to fall short in our prayer life, to be faithful to it no matter what state our soul may be in.

During these next two weeks then, let's improve our prayer in the ways I mentioned and in what seems most useful to all of us.

To improve our prayer life!

The first Christians who had just begun to grasp the message of Jesus, and knew what demands it contained, gave great importance to prayer. We must imitate them.

In this way we will become worthy of the Ideal, our Holy Journey will be on its way, we will draw many graces for ourselves, and we will delude neither God, nor the Pope.

To improve. May this verb, this thrust, become a necessity for us, an interior attitude, an aid to our spiritual life without which we cannot live. In doing so, we will be at the height of what we should be, which is to be members of the Work of Mary in whom the Holy Father places so much hope.

October 3, 1985

To Overcome

With the arrival of October, our new "ideal year"[24] has begun. Since once in a while we must stop for a moment to see how we are progressing on our Holy Journey, I think this may be a good moment to do so. As we know, in our Holy Journey we aim for sanctity. But we can only truly aim for sanctity if it is a goal that we definitely hope to achieve. To launch ourselves toward its conquest, we need, in fact, to believe that such an undertaking is possible. And I think that this hope does lie in the hearts of us all.

All the same, there may be some among us who do not see it in this way. Perhaps because too much thought may be given to sins from the past, or to the slow pace of one's correspondence up until this point. There is a danger then, to be resigned to a mediocre life.

This is a serious mistake.

In whatever situation we may now find ourselves, we must be sure that we will make it. There are three reasons to be encouraged: first of all there is this month's Word of Life: "To God, everything is possible" (Mk 10:27). Then there are the saints. In fact, those whom we see to have been canonized have not always been so saintly. Let's recall St. Jerome who, crouched under the weight of his sins, had heard the Lord tell him, "Give your sins to Me." Let's think of St. Augustine, of Blessed Angela of Foligno, of St. Ignatius of Loyola, of St. Teresa of Avila herself, who even though she hadn't committed grave sins, throughout her whole lifetime she sensed the weight of her initial lack of response to God.

---

[24] *The beginning of a year's sequence of activity and spiritual guidelines is marked by an October general meeting of all those responsible for various geographical zones and particular endeavors of the Focolare.*

Then there is a third reason that gives us hope: our brothers and sisters who have recently completed their Holy Journey. In fact, many of them have made it; their lives' conclusions were stupendous. And I am not speaking only of Luminosa and of Margrit, but of others who may be less known to us, but not to God. Those who have been close to them have assured me that these marvelous passages to the Heavenly Mariapolis are not exceptions in the Work of Mary.

They made it; so therefore, we can make it too.

We need to have faith, and not see any possible future except that of becoming saints, instruments of God for the salvation of many. This is certainly what God wants from us. Everything else is a product of our own thoughts, human reasoning, and impressions.

But how can we reach such heights? In the meantime, every time we are taken by discouragement because it appears impossible for us to reach the goal of sanctity, instead of hesitating, we must tell Jesus that we thank Him for His work in digging the foundations of humility in our souls, the necessary premise for sanctity; we must tell Him that we are joyful because nothing is more important to us than to see ourselves in every moment of life similar to Him forsaken; that we wouldn't exchange these moments with any other because it is He who is important to us, He whom we have chosen.

In this way, the Risen Lord takes hold within us and with Him there is the certainty that, even though we may not be aware of it, He is pulling us away from a Christian life which may be tepid, to bring us into the spheres of His fire. The hope of becoming saints will reappear, and even more so, of becoming great saints for the benefit of many; and with a greater sense of trust, we will direct all our joys, sorrows, and conquests toward achieving this goal.

I read a book that is about to be published concerning our trip to Asia in 1981,[25] the first year of our Holy Journey, and I was able to see with what thrust we began our journey to sanctity.

---

[25] *Chiara Lubich,* Incontri con l'Oriente, *Rome, 1986, pp. 248*

A desire invaded my heart that this new year be like that first one—and even better. The fact is that the helmsman of our ship was Jesus Forsaken. We didn't see anything but Him, and possessed nothing but Him.

Our hope lies in the fact that everything is possible to Him; and if, because this is so, we must expect much on the part of God, we must also do our own part.

My invitation then would be that we begin again to follow Jesus Forsaken. He shows us how Christianity is not something static, but dynamic. Jesus Forsaken does not hesitate in the situations in which He finds Himself, but overcomes all things. He overcomes the impression and temptation of thinking that He has been abandoned by God; He overcomes the sensation of the nothingness and emptiness which envelops Him; He overcomes the fear, anguish, and doubt that take hold of Him, the weakness He feels, the discouragement that swept over Him, the distance from His Father that He feels, and He lives all the virtues in the most heroic manner.

In following Him we must do the same: overcome each suffering by accepting it always, immediately and with joy; and to live with the greatest effort all that the voice of the Spirit within our hearts asks of us.

To overcome, overcome, overcome. To go beyond. To remind ourselves that Christianity calls for a dynamic life because it is a life of love.

"To overcome" is our watch-word for these next two weeks, in order to keep traveling ahead on the way of sanctity.

October 17, 1985

Let's Keep Jesus in our Midst

"To love God...and our neighbor...is worth more than all offerings and sacrifices" (Mk 12:33). This is the warning that this month's Word of Life gives us. And we know that the concrete way to love God is to love our neighbor. Therefore, love for our neighbor is worth more than all offerings and sacrifices.

Perhaps we can see now why the Focolare has been given many blessings from Heaven and receives so much providence from God. It is because it has centered on what is of most value: love, and in particular, love of neighbor; it has made love its road to God, its objective. Our goal, in fact, is the perfection of charity.

Then we also have a specific goal: to work toward fulfilling the Testament of Jesus, which means opening ourselves toward the various dialogues to be established. But all our activities have significance for us if love of neighbor is at their foundation.

Love of neighbor. Someone could make an objection saying that this is the general goal of all the works of the Church. This is certainly so. But even though love of neighbor is the general goal of every religious family, we—since the Holy Spirit uses infinite imagination to shape His works—have a particular way of loving our neighbor, and therefore a way of our own to please God more than by offering holocausts and sacrifices.

We love our neighbors to the point of achieving unity with them. We must love by loving one another; we must love in unity, and therefore we must have Jesus in our midst.

Jesus in our midst, unity, is our way to live in order to be true members of the Focolare. When in the early days of the Focolare we were asked whether we had thought of wearing a badge (at that time it was customary in Catholic associations to do so), we would say that our badge was reciprocal love; and if in some moments we found ourselves to be lacking this love, we no longer felt part of the Focolare.

Yes, this is it: it is this badge that is so evangelical in nature that it must distinguish us as members of the Focolare. In this case, it shouldn't do any harm to make a few comments on this task of ours. Are we today, this very moment, in the most perfect unity with those whom we know in the Focolare?

If our answer is yes, let's thank God and be assured that all that we do—even the smallest of things—as washing dishes, or sweeping a room, or waking up the children or doing some shopping, reading a book or taking a walk, even a smile, a gesture, a sentiment... everything, everything has value, and thus more reason still, working for the Work of Mary, carrying out its many activities. Doesn't St. Paul say that charity gives value to all things?

If our answer is no, our first duty is to recompose a unity that may be a bit cloudy, or worse, cracked or broken.

The Statutes of the Work of Mary, in which the life of all its internal members is described, contains a premise which is the norm of all norms, without which none of the others have any value. This premise states that before everything else we must establish the presence of Jesus among us through mutual love.

I know that I am telling you very simple things, but they demand the highest attention. Woe to me if I didn't say these things! I would be failing to carry out the primary task that God has entrusted to me.

And woe to all of you if you don't do everything possible to put them into practice! They are required by the charism with which you have been invested.

Is the situation in that nucleus, or that Gen unit, or in that headquarters of the Focolare, or that family-focolare at a standstill? Is the light of Jesus in our midst, and that ardor with which he enflames hearts, and the enthusiasm of the early days missing? Let's be straightforward and give ourselves the blame that we haven't been vigilant in love. Let's leave every other activity in order to establish first the presence of Jesus in our midst. When this is done, everything is done. It is something very urgent to take care of; it is our duty to do so. Bring back the presence of Jesus in your midst, and He will show you again the splendor of the Work of Mary; He will take you by the hand and teach you to walk; He will reveal to you once again the fascination of the divine adventure that you had undertaken in His name.

Is this work costly? But haven't we perhaps consecrated ourselves various times to Jesus Forsaken, with the decision to take upon our shoulders, above all, the crosses of imperfect unity so that the Risen Lord may be triumphant among us? Haven't we seen Him and followed Him for the very reason that He is the key to every unity? Are we now stepping back because we find this task costly?

No. I am sure that you understand me, and that you will act upon my proposal.

God demands it, and Our Lady wants it. To live with Jesus in our midst gives body to the Focolare. It keeps it alive.

And you want the Focolare, which is yours, to be so.

Christmas is coming. Wouldn't it be right to begin now to prepare a beautiful gift the size of the world (since the Focolare is all over the world) for the Child Jesus who came to earth so that all may be one?

Let's begin from this very moment to replenish our lives with new light by reviving His presence among us.

The purpose of the Holy Journey that we are undertaking together is to become saints. But we will never arrive at this objective if we do not live in such a way that the Saint may live among us.

It is because of His presence, the extent of His presence that some of our members have passed on into the Heavenly Mariapolis as saints.

Our watch-word therefore for the next two weeks: to establish the presence of Jesus in our midst with all those who live the Ideal with us; to live in a way that when we greet each other we would want to spontaneously tell each other "Let's keep Jesus in our midst."

November 6, 1985

Listen to the Voice of the Holy Spirit

I feel that all of you — because many of you have confirmed it to me — are committed to preparing the "big gift" for the Child Jesus. Christmas is drawing near and on that day we would want the presence of Jesus in our midst in every branch or component of the Focolare to have grown significantly. In fact, we have understood, still once again, that the Focolare wasn't primarily born for the extensive goals of the Work of Mary, which fascinate us just the same and for which I too day by day notice special graces; its primary purpose is to be perfect in love, in charity.

Therefore, I would like to say a few words about this also in this conference call in order that we might better reach this general goal of ours, through which we can truly establish and maintain the presence of Jesus among the members of the focolare centers, in the nucleuses, in the Gen units and in all of our communities.

To be perfect in love. To reach this goal — as we know — each day we must become more perfect, because "those who don't go ahead, go backwards." Love for the person alongside of us must always be more refined.

But what is the best means to achieve such an objective?

I don't see other means than to direct our heart, mind and strength toward Jesus Forsaken with a constant desire to renew our love for Him; to love Him in the inevitable sufferings of each day, in the practice of the virtues, in the mortifications that we are called to practice as Christians and as members of the Work of Mary. It is this love — as we say — this always going beyond the wound in each moment, that allows the Risen Lord to live in us in a luminous way and the Spirit to break all the chains of our ego. And if the Spirit is freed within us, He will be able to increase the charity that He Himself has infused in our hearts.

During these last few days I have been experiencing that in trying to live with the Risen Lord in my heart, the voice of God grows more pronounced within me and it is this voice that guides me in all the relationships that I must establish, with whomever I meet.

How often perhaps would I add an extra word or leave one out if I wasn't attentive to that resonant voice, and therefore threaten to weaken our present dialogue with the Buddhists that appears so promising.

Yes, we cannot improvise charity which is a participation in the divine life; we must draw it from God and from His Spirit. Therefore, when we listen to and obey His voice, the plan of God unfolds in a magnificent way. And as this happens, unity among us grows and deepens, bringing us closer to that reality of preparing this "big gift" for Him.

We have an ideal that is both extraordinary and divine. As I read the messages that arrive from all over the world, my soul is deeply moved: how much grace lies in all of our souls, what abundance God has poured out for you! The young and the mature are all filled with this charism of God! We truly do not know what we have. Better yet, we do know: we have Jesus, the Son of God in and among us who lives and reigns where charity is queen. Therefore, so that this may always be so, so that the reality of this miracle of love which the Focolare is may always grow stronger, let's make a renewed effort to love Jesus Forsaken in order that the Risen Lord may radiate within our hearts. The voice of His Spirit will strengthen within us and we will be able to be always more perfect in love, always more pleasing to God and to Mary, and then always more fit to serve the Church.

Let's keep this trinominal in mind: Jesus Forsaken, the Risen Lord, and to listen to the voice of the Holy Spirit. If we do this, we will be an expression of God's love for everyone.

November 21, 1985

To Grow and to Be Overabundant

The Word of Life for this month is truly fabulous, and it will be helpful for many of us.

In fact, we must admit that even with all our good will, the journey to sanctity is not an easy one.

Moreover, it would be outside the normality of things if from time to time we were not faced with a difficult situation, a temptation, or the impression of no longer being able to make it. It happens to everyone, and we shouldn't be taken by surprise. The very lives of the saints are marked by trials that occur one after the other.

For us who for the most part live in the midst of the world, there is even more reason for this to be true.

The world — as we know — even in its undeniable beauties which merit all of our attention and appreciation (for its progess, its various cultures, its new discoveries, its natural richness, humankind's many inventions) is still the number one danger for a Christian. It is the environment in which Satan reigns with all his deceptions, his seductions, attractions and perverse offers. And Christians who live in this environment are called day by day to go against the current, to keep their distances, and to defend themselves. And they do not always succeed in doing so. Interior struggles are unleashed, and why not? Concrete persecutions arrive from those who do not think the same way as we do. We could feel driven to abandon our Holy Journey, to set it aside and to coast into the road of mediocrity.

But we cannot do it. We cannot betray Jesus who has filled our hearts with such joy in exchange for even the little we have done in answering His call. Even if moments come in which we would want to cry "enough," causing us to want to give up our struggle, we feel we cannot surrender. What must we hold onto to keep us from falling away? What is the medicine or the remedy which we can rely on in these kinds of moments which all of us must pass through?

The remedy lies in the Word of Life for this month. It is truly a fabulous and extraordinary one. I have tried to put it into practice and it appears to me — the saints would say — as a *sanatotum* (cure-all), which restores health to everything. St. Paul wrote this to the Thessalonians, a young community whose strength was threatened by persecution. He did not find a better cure than making this suggestion: to grow and be overabundant in love for one another and for everyone.

Reciprocal love, therefore, and love for all.

The Apostle Paul knew that if there was reciprocal love, Jesus would be present among those Christians who were tempted to surrender; and if they were faithful in loving the others, the Lord would have dwelled in their hearts. Therefore he affirms, and this is our Word of Life for the month, "May the Lord make you grow and be overabundant in your love for one another and for everyone (1 Th 3:12)

"To grow and be overabundant."

This is the cure also for those of us who are undergoing difficult moments.

This is a Word of Life for all of us who in various parts of the day face the possibility of falling out of tune.

Try it. Try to grow and be overabundant in love. Before writing this conference call, I too have tried to do this, and I found myself in such peace. I had the impression that this is a Word of Life that enters the deepest region of our hearts. It is our very charism. To encourage each other to do so would be to touch on the very essence of our life.

Try in the meantime to grow in reciprocal love with those who share our Ideal, and you will realize how sweet and pleasant is its application. At times it will mean to say an extra word, give an extra smile, to be a bit more attentive, to make a gift which otherwise we would not have done.

Try to concentrate your lives solely on this growing and being overabundant, and you will experience new life flowing within your souls, while fears, doubts, sensations of feeling blocked and restrained, temptations, or whatever they are, will begin to vanish.

This Word of Life works the miracle of our continual

rebirth: through a faith that is more alive, a hope that is more secure and a charity that is more ardent, the Risen Lord will shine forth always more resplendently within us. In this there is life.

Try it and you will experience that you are on course. The mortifications and penances that we must practice in order to love our ideal, Jesus Forsaken, are implicit in this growing and being overabundant, and therefore they are typically our own.

But let's not limit ourselves to loving only those who share our ideal. Let's love everyone. This is what the Gospel asks of us.

Let's grow and be overabundant in love also towards every neighbor, and in a few minutes, I assure you, also those who feel defeated will acquire new trust and will experience once again to be journeying towards our goal with the same enthusiasm of the journey's start.

Then there is the "big gift" that we want to prepare for Christmas. What better Word of Life could be offered to us?

With the heart of St. Paul I would like to wish all of you and myself that our community which is spread throughout the world may grow and be overabundant in charity to the extent of truly giving joy to Jesus in Heaven, causing Him to say: This is truly the most beautiful Christmas since the day I was born on earth.

Therefore, so that this may become true, let's remember: to grow and to be overabundant in love.

December 5, 1985

The Experience of God

As you know, I recently made that strong experience of Church at the Synod.[26] You will be informed during the year on how the Synod went, what topics it treated, and the consequences that we, as the Focolare, must draw from this event.

In this conference call I would like to mention another experience that I have made parallel to the one made at the Synod.

We spent two weeks at the Vatican and each day I encountered cardinals and bishops who expressed to me their appreciation for the Focolare. In fact, two thirds of those present knew about it. This was an occasion for me to see the Work of Mary as truly a Work of God spread out through all the earth, so beautiful and dignified (there were some who used such superlative expressions to define it), so rooted now in the Church, that it appeared to me as a blossoming of the tree of this century's Church. And I had the net sensation that it was something far beyond our every imagination, surpassing our very selves, and all of us put together. In fact, I had the impression that all its members were merely poor and simple instruments of the Work of Mary, like brushes or paint colors, and then the impression of contemplating and admiring the stupendous painting the true Artist-God had composed.

But why is the Work of Mary so beautiful? What specific quality does it have which renders it so acceptable to the bishops of the Church that they feel it as their own?

I believe the reason lies in that this Work of God has been conceived in such a way by the Holy Spirit that it puts people

---

[26]*Refers to the extraordinary Synod of Bishops held in October of 1985 in view of the twentieth anniversary of Vatican Council II in which the author participated as an observer.*

into contact with God, and places them in the condition of experiencing God.

When, because we have embraced the cross, we are overwhelmed by the gifts of the Spirit which are peace, light, love, joy... isn't it God, Jesus, the Risen Lord whom we experience and whom the others see in us?

When reciprocal love is lived, isn't it Jesus, alive in our midst, whom we experience? Isn't He the one whom others meet when they come into contact with us, and in their turn, make this same experience?

But it is precisely because they either directly or indirectly make this experience of God that persons who are far from Him accept as logical, almost with rationalizing, everything that lies behind this experience: the Christian life with all of its demands, the Sacred Scriptures with all of its commandments, the Sacraments, the Church with its hierarchy, etc. They accept all things whose purpose is to draw people to God, to allow them to make the experience of God and His kingdom.

And since all these things are accepted wholeheartedly and are entirely identified with, the bishops notice that the members of the Work of Mary are "one" with the Church, and at the same time they witness its apostolic influence also upon the atheistic and secularized world which gives them a sense of joy and satisfaction for which in turn they bestow many blessings on our work.

And we, for our part, are deeply consoled by their blessings. In fact, it seems to us, and it is true, that if the Holy Father and the bishops are happy with our work, then Jesus Himself is happy also. However, if the case were otherwise, it would not be so.

Therefore, if the Church approves our work through their blessings, what conclusion must we draw? What direction must we give to our life? It's obvious: to *be* (as many of her representatives tell us) *ourselves,* to live our vocation with an always greater totality.

So during the remainder of December, we must practice the Word of Life better, which is so in tune with our life, so central to our spirituality, but whose richness can never be exhausted: to grow and to be overabundant in reciprocal love and in love for everyone.

Stay anchored in this Word of Life as if it were our salvation, as if it were the key to open our way to sanctity.

During these past two weeks we must have certainly grown in love. But the Word of Life asks us to grow still more and always; moreover, to even be overabundant, meaning not to place limits on our reciprocal love and on our love for everyone.

Let's live in this way and our "big gift" for Jesus will become a reality. Best wishes to everyone: love, love, love, and with love may you bring the world to experience God, who is Love.

December 19, 1985

To Be His Witnesses

We begin the new year (the sixth of our Holy Journey) with another splendid Word of Life: "You will be my witnesses in Jerusalem, in all of Judea and Samaria until the ends of the earth" (Ac 1:8).

"You will be my witnesses...until the ends of the earth." With these words Jesus concluded one of His last encounters with the Apostles after the Resurrection.

He had probably spoken to them about the coming of the Holy Spirit and now was clarifying for them that He would come not for performing a spectacular change in society, as they would expect, but to transform their persons, so that they might give witness to Him, bringing the Risen Lord within themselves to the ends of the earth.

Bringing the Risen Lord. Yes, because in order to bear witness to God, we must demonstrate that He exists, that He lives, and that He is the Living One. Nothing then is more useful to bear witness to God, the Living One, than to bring Him alive in ourselves, as the Risen Lord.

Once they received the Holy Spirit, this is what the Apostles did.

But, as we know, the Holy Spirit has been given to us as far back as our baptism. Therefore these words are also for us: "You will be my witnesses...until the ends of the earth."

Witnesses. Do you know what the greek word for "witness" is? *Martýrion.*

The martyrs, in fact, are considered to be the first witnesses.

But also other ways we know which give witness to Jesus demand martyrdom.

We must die to ourselves by embracing Jesus Forsaken so that the Risen Lord may live in each one of us.

We also need to be dead to ourselves so that the Risen Lord may be resplendent among us. And we know that when He is among us we bear witness to Him. Didn't Jesus pray that they may be one so that the world may believe (cf. Jn 17:21)? In other words: that they may be one so the world may see a witness of Me and then believe.

To allow the Risen Lord to live in us and among us are the two ways with which the Holy Spirit has taught us to bear witness.

During these next two weeks we could aim at the first way.

How then can we live in such a way that this becomes true?

What aspect of our life can we give special attention to?

If we take a look at our lifestyle according to the Ideal that God has given us, we see that everyday each one of us follows more or less diligently our planned program: the accomplishment of various tasks, an appointment with someone, letters to be written, a discourse to be outlined. Time is taken out for meals, for rest and maybe for relaxation also. And if the persons who planned the programs are faithful to them and in all good will live in the thrust towards sanctity, they perform everything to perfection, recognizing Jesus in the neighbors they meet, keeping Him alive among all.

However, each day always brings something unforeseen: small or big changes that alter our plans; and these too are the will of God for us. No day passes which does not find one or more unforeseen elements being added into our program which can partially or even entirely change it.

Naturally if we are truly attentive to the voice of the Holy Spirit within us, we know how to receive with love each piece of news, each circumstance, each encounter, each event.

If, instead, we are not very attentive to the voice of the Spirit, we remain attached to our programs and we do not know how to allow our own wills to die in the will of God. In moments like these, the light of the Risen Lord dies out in us.

Therefore, in the next two weeks, in order to be able to bear witness to Jesus always, we must pay special attention to what may arrive outside of our established program. Our own constant reminder that we have all offered ourselves to Jesus Forsaken will be of great assistance to us. The abandonment on the part of the Father was not in Jesus' program, at least for what we may know. Yet, it was foreseen by the Father to complete the Passion of His Son so that He might free humankind from sin.

But Jesus, after His surprising cry, "My God, my God, why have you forsaken me?" immediately accepts this frightening circumstance that was not in His expectations and trustingly says, "Father, into your hands I commend my spirit."

Likewise, we must also be ready for all the unforeseen things that could happen during the day, and—whether it be something pleasant, or painful or indifferent—we must make it immediately our own so that the Risen Lord, the Living One, may shine incessantly within our hearts.

In this way we will truly bear witness to Him.

January 2, 1986

100%

As we all know, our Ideal can be defined with one single word: love.

Our entire life is love. The soul of our prayer, of our apostolate and of all the various aspects of our existence, is love.

The health of our individual spiritual life is love, as our health as a community and as the mystical Body of Christ, is reciprocal love. In fact, when we love, we lack nothing; we are completely whole before God, whether we may be enjoying good physical health or whether we are ill.

But it is easy to love when we are healthy; it is easy to love God and our neighbors. It is more difficult to love when we are not physically well.

Few times have I seen lived this love we ought to have in our sicknesses as I have seen in these past few days. Few times has someone with a grave sickness made me want to say when looking at her, "How healthy she is!"

As you can imagine, every so often I go to visit Marilen[27] at the Mariapolis Center where she is spending this particular period of her sickness, and the impression that I gather is that she is a truly healthy person, completely healthy. Her body is certainly not healthy, but her soul is healthy, fully healthy.

It is true that when we consecrate ourselves to Jesus Forsaken, we can welcome His various visits with 20%, 50%, 70%, or with 100% of our heart and will.

Marilen welcomes Him with 100%. Her life is a continual "for You," meaning that she offers everything to Him for us, for the Work of God.

---

[27] *Maria Elena Holzhauser, one of the author's first companions, who in that period of time was gravely ill.*

I mention this beautiful example of Marilen's life in order to place myself and now you before this question: Is it right that a person who finds herself in such difficult moments of her earthly life live her soul's espousal to Jesus Forsaken with such great conviction, while we who perhaps have better physical health may be living our thrust toward sanctity in a very mediocre way? Do we always have to wait for God to permit special trials in our regard, those that seem to take away our very breath, in order to make us decide to love Him totally.

No, we have begun the sixth year of our Holy Journey and we must put ourselves into the disposition to live it in full stride.

Someone mentioned to me that it could be considered as the first year. I would advise you to consider it as our last, as if it were the year in which we decide before God whether we will or will not become saints.

Then, if we do think of it in this way (and who can say that it won't be so?) we cannot lose time.

We all have the Holy Spirit in our hearts, and we know what He requires and points out to us. For example, in a suffering that we encounter it is He who tells us: here you must love Jesus Forsaken; or in an increased effort to be made: here you must prefer Him in a particular virtue; in love of neighbor: here still you must choose Him present in a particular aspect of the Work of Mary, or of the Church or of humanity itself....

We must make the resolution to love Him always 100%, day in and day out as Marilen does. And like her, before each one of our actions we must repeat, "for You."

If such a committed life should frighten us (the devil is capable of doing all kinds of things to discourage us), let's recall, as Marilen does, the words of Jesus: "Today has troubles enough of its own" (Mt 6:34). Therefore, let's recognize and live for the countenance of Jesus Forsaken who comes before us today and in each moment. For tomorrow, we will have other graces.

In this way we will accumulate a collection of fully lived days, all consecrated to Him. It is with these days that we will build our sanctity.

If it happens that we fail, betray, or become restrained, we know that behind these circumstances we can find His countenance.

My wish is that each evening we might be able to answer to ourselves, or better to Jesus who from deep within our hearts asks us about how our day was, "It went well, I lived it 100%."

In this way we will also live the Word of Life of the month: "You will be my witnesses."

By embracing Jesus Forsaken 100%, the Risen Lord shines in us, among us, and gives witness.

So then, can we make this agreement? Let's compete with Marilen, that for the next 350 days (the remaining days of the year) we might always be able to say in the evening: 100%.

January 16, 1986

To Be Vigilant

Among the many members of the Work of Mary who listened to the last conference call, there was also Sebastiano Biarese, a wonderful Volunteer who was responsible for the nucleus of Mondovì in northern Italy. He was 39 years old and recently attended a meeting at Sassone (Rome).

When the meeting was over, he returned home that Sunday evening and stayed awake until one o'clock in the morning speaking about that meeting with his wife, Meri, a delegate of the Volunteer women. They also made the resolution to love Jesus Forsaken 100%, as we said last time.

He had also decided not to buy a house in order to be free to relocate into another area whenever the Work of Mary would see fit. At mass the morning after, as if for the last time, both of them renewed the same promise to live 100%. On that very same day, he really did relocate to another place, a very special one: struck by an electric current, Sebastiano left for the Heavenly Mariapolis.

Why am I telling you about this fact? Certainly not to make you sad, nor to frighten you even though the fear of God is a healthy attitude.

I told you about what happened to Sebastiano because the purpose of our conference calls is to bring us always closer to being a single family, a single focolare throughout the whole world; to share amongst all our joys, sorrows, hopes and projects so that in unity we may find the strength to reach sanctity. I told you this also so that Meri and her fine son may in this difficult moment experience our deepest unity, our most Christian solidarity.

Then we would like to praise God together and thank Him for having taken to Himself a member of our family in such a beautiful moment.

And lastly, we would want to better understand how the

things of God are terribly serious, and that we cannot treat Him in a joking manner. We cannot take God lightly. In fact, He forewarned us.

Didn't He caution us saying, "Keep your eyes open, for you know not the day nor the hour" (Mt 25:13)?

If what had happened to our Volunteer should personally happen to each one of us, we could not complain. Therefore, we must really put ourselves into the train of thought indicated by Jesus.

As you know, the Word of Life for this month of February which enlightens our journey advises: "Not on bread alone shall man live" (Lk 4:4). True, because man lives also by the Word of God.

And which Word of Life should we emphasize during these next two weeks.

I would really suggest: "Keep your eyes open, for you know not the day nor the hour."

Therefore: to be vigilant. But what does it mean to be vigilant. It means to be very cautious, to stay alert, to keep our eyes open. It means, then, to be very present in each minute of time.

I have seen through my own experience that we can be very vigilant when we decide to live the will of God fully, each of us projected into His will in the present moment.

Living in this way, we capture the moment, each moment of God. We cannot hold off this most important task of ours to be vigilant until later, or until tomorrow, or the day after tomorrow. If Sebastiano had not immediately decided to love Jesus as if it were the last chance he had to love Him, perhaps we couldn't be joyful today concerning his death.

No: we must always stay alert. In this way, He will always find us with our lamps lit, the lamps of the oil of love.

Therefore, let's make this resolution: to be attentive to what God wants from us in the present moment and embrace it.

In this way, we will truly be vigilant. And in whatever moment He comes, under the form of suffering, joy, or even death, He will find us ready.

Let's be vigilant then, fully living the present moment.

February 6, 1986

Perfect Works out of Love for Jesus Forsaken

The longing for sanctity that overwhelms us at times (and if our hearts do not sense this we must through prayer ask the Holy Spirit for it and He will not leave us without it) often brings us to ask ourselves to what foothold, what support, to what rope must we grasp onto in order to walk surefootedly alongside the world that lies below, which is wounded and often dying because of the materialism that has invaded it, the secularism, hedonism and religious indifference that reigns within it.

And immediately a very well known name reappeared in my soul: Jesus Forsaken. Therefore, to grasp onto Jesus Forsaken. To love Jesus Forsaken.

It is this name that touches upon so many aspects of our individual and collective life, that I would also like to expound on a bit today.

To be more precise, I would like to tell you something about a particular way of loving Jesus Forsaken, who is the gateway and road to sanctity.

I told you one day that the great act of love that Jesus asks of us is to work for the Focolare, which is His Work.

Today I would like to point out to you that this work for the Work of Mary is not a vague love for God, but it is precisely love for Jesus Forsaken.

During these last few days we have been preparing the meeting for the Parish Movement that will be held on the third and fourth of May in the Paul VI auditorium at the Vatican in Rome.

As have many others, I too have gotten myself involved in its preparation. Now, as I am writing discourses, listening to other ones, and correcting experiences, I understand better how the success of that day will depend very much on how we prepare each detail now and how we will present it then.

Did we prepare each speaker well?

Have we taken care of every detail to perfection, to the point that the Spirit in our hearts has nothing more to suggest to us? Will we act in the same way on the day of the meeting? If so, we can be assured that everything will go well, that with the help of God there will be a blaze of love. We can be certain that the impact of this meeting will be felt for a long time and its effects will cover a wide radius of territory. We can then be sure that the life of this structural unit of the Church, the parish, whose life is at times neglected or even non-existent, will return vibrantly.

We can be sure that the countenance of Jesus Forsaken that we recognize in this aspect of the Church will be soothed, consoled, and made more beautiful in many parts of the world.

In this way we will love Jesus Forsaken.

But it is not only in working for the Parish Movement that we will love Jesus Forsaken.

Are we involved in the New Families Movement? Doesn't the family today often remind us of the disfigured countenance of Jesus Forsaken, the one who is divided, separated, or destroyed? Do we work within the Youth for a United World Movement? Aren't our youth often another expression of the countenance of Jesus Forsaken through all the problems that assail them: delusion, indifference, mistrust, and unemployment?

Do we work within the various worlds of New Humanity? Do we not find many situations in the health field, in politics, education, the mass media, the economy, that remind us of the one we love?

I could go on, but you understand what I'm saying.

Wherever in the Work of Mary we go, we can find His countenance, we can hear his cry.

Wherever we look, we have the marvelous opportunity to love Him, to comfort Him, to find solutions to specific problems which are all expressions of Him. And this is quite a grace. Through our work, we are always in contact with Him, with Jesus Forsaken, and by loving Him we can build our sanctification.

However, there are different measures of love for Him. We

can love Him greatly, or we can love Him little. And this means that with our love for Him we can contribute toward our great sanctity or toward a small one. There are activities that we carry out in the Focolare that once completed, are no longer necessary. There is no doubt that also through them we have in some way loved Jesus Forsaken. But some of our activities are ones that are always needed, which in general are the ones that are most useful and successful.

We need to accomplish works that remain, that will always have something to give. In this way our love for Jesus Forsaken will be great.

The saints have searched and are searching for the love which renders the most benefit for the glory of God.

Are we writing our personal life story in order to share our experience?

Let's do it well, very well, listening with great love to the voice inside of us which sheds light on our past and present, a light which others would appreciate hearing about because it is attractive.

Let's pay close attention to what that voice suggests to us and to what corrections He makes.

Let's pour our greatest efforts into everything we do.

Let's continue to correct our work until that voice has no more to tell us.

We must never mistreat the Work of God. We must never do imperfect works.

Therefore, let's do everything well, very well.

So then our proposal for the next two weeks: for every work that we take up, let's try to discover which countenance of Jesus Forsaken we can love in doing so, and then accomplish it perfectly.

Therefore, perfect works out of love for Jesus Forsaken. This is the way to build our sanctity, our great sanctity.

February 20, 1986

To Be Reborn through Love

Here we are, linked up once again in order to travel together on our journey towards sanctity.

Easter by now is right around the corner, but we are still in Lent. As we know, the Lenten season asks all Christians to make a conversion.

So this is true also for us.

And what is the typical conversion that we, who are members of the Focolare, must be ready to make, particularly during the season of Lent?

This "converging" and redirecting of our lives toward God finds its most concrete application in our turning towards our neighbor, in the consideration of our neighbor as our specific means toward approaching God. You know how often we speak of our neighbors and of the love we owe them. However, each time we are enlightened about this, it appears as something new to us.

A few days ago it also happened to me.

I was reading the daily Missalette for meditation and the stupendous page on the final judgment appeared before me: "Jesus who will come to judge us and tell us '...I was hungry and you gave me to eat, I was thirsty and you gave me to drink...' (Mt 25:35)."

It was as if I was reading those words for the first time. I rediscovered that in the final judgment Jesus will not ask me if I did this or that thing which I must do anyway, but He will aim directly at love for neighbor.

Like a person who was just beginning her ascent to God, I began to love everyone, everyone who in one way or another crossed my path during the day. And believe me, I felt as if I were reborn. I reminded myself that my soul, above all, thirsts for love, thirsts to love, and that it is in love towards everyone where it truly finds its rest, its nourishment and its life. It is true that I had previously tried to perform many acts of charity, but I now realize that some of them were stemming from an excessively individualistic spirituality, fed by small or larger penances; which, notwithstanding our good will, can become an occasion for us who are called to love, to look upon our own selves instead. Now, in this new effort to love everyone, I could still perform many acts of charity but they would all be for the service of my neighbors in whom I could see and love Jesus. And it was only in this way that I could experience fullness of joy.

We are called to continually work at our own reconversion; we must all experience this kind of rebirth, this fullness of life. Therefore we must try as much as possible to translate all the aspects of our daily existence into charity towards our neighbor.

Is it our task to keep up the house? Let's not do so for merely human reasons, but because there is Jesus in the others to be loved by dressing, feeding and serving them. Do we have any other kind of responsibility to take care of? Jesus is present in the individuals and in the communities whom we serve. Must we pray? Let's always pray for the others as well as ourselves, referring to that "we" that Jesus has taught us to use in the "Our Father." Are we called to suffer? Let's offer our suffering for the others. Is it the will of God to spend time with someone? Let's always have the intention to listen to Him, to give advice to Him, to console Him...in short: to love Him. Must we rest, eat, or take out time for recreation? In all these actions let's place the intention of wanting to regather our strength in order to serve our neighbor better.

In other words, let's do all things with our neighbor in mind.

And even though this spiritual attitude which brings us constantly outside of ourselves will be a source of great joy (I mentioned rebirth), nevertheless we can be sure that the effort involved in going out of ourselves to "live the others," as we say, will be present.

Through this effort we will be offered the possiblility of loving Jesus Forsaken in the practice of the virtues of patience, benevolence, humility, magnanimity, poverty, and purity which are all implicit in charity.

Yes, we must become saints, but through the road indicated for us: the way of love, a radical love which first of all must be lived among us where it is reciprocal, and then with everyone.

So that such a continual conversion may take place in us, during the next two weeks let's keep in mind our commitment "to be reborn through love."

Doing so, we will prepare ourselves for Easter, a feast day for which I wish all of you the joy of full resurrection, assuring you that I will be living the teachings and mysteries of the preceding Holy Week in perfect unity with each of you: the New Commandment, the Testament of Jesus, the institution of the priesthood, the Eucharist, and the cry of Jesus, "My God, my God, why have you forsaken me?" (Mt 27:46).

March 20, 1986

Unceasing Love for Him

Easter has gone by and has left all of us, I think, with a vivid meditation on the Risen Lord who must live in and among us.

As it was for Jesus, so for the Focolare, this extraordinary event has been preceded by a profound meditation on death. This was given to us by Marilen, who left this earth fourteen days ago.

You will receive material which gives an account of the very rich life of hers, and of her death which has been just as rich. Today, however, I would like to at least mention a few words about her.

At a certain point in her life, Marilen had asked Jesus for the grace to go through her purgatory while here on earth, and it truly seems that her wish was fulfilled.

In fact, it appeared during these last few months that God was asking from her, as He did from Job, one thing after another of all which He had given her in life. She had lost the use of her legs (she could no longer stand up), the use of her hands (she could no longer hold onto anything), the use of speech (she could hardly say a word); it was extremely difficult for her to breathe, her memory was even failing her, and at the end she could no longer swallow. She was approaching her last day.

When she realized this fact — it was the evening before she went into a deep sleep — she had asked a Focolarina who was caring for her to advise me that she was at the point of death and I then told her, "Marilen, Jesus is asking many things from you; give all of them to Him generously." She responded, "Yes." I continued, "Marilen, love Jesus Forsaken beyond all reason." She answered, "Yes."

She was able to say yes in that moment because she had done so in all that was requested of her beforehand.

What was most striking in this last period of Marilen's life was to see that God can ask a person for one thing after another without letting up, and that she could have the grace to always say yes.

To those who visited her, such a witness was an inspiration which gave rise to ardent desires and a few questions; even though we are not in the same condition as Marilen, why should we wait for the announcement of our approaching death to place ourselves in the disposition to love Him? Why not begin right away to do so, saying yes unceasingly to all the demands of His love. Why wait to love Him out of fear of death, and not love Him immediately out of love. Don't all of us, young and old, have to die? Wouldn't it be better to immediately keep this reality in mind, and thrust ourselves into an unceasing ascent?

Yes, these are the questions that were raised in our hearts while Marilen, nailed upon the cross, took us along with her. We wanted to respond to these questions and still want to do so together with you in order to share with you this great gift of ours of having lived, together with Marilen, the final moments of her earthly adventure.

We know for Whom we must live our life. We know where we can find Jesus Forsaken who awaits our love.

He is right there in all the painful circumstances of life, in the sacrifices which reciprocal love brings, in the mortifications implicit in our Christian and Ideal life, in our work for the Work of Mary, which is all projected toward relieving the sufferings of Jesus Forsaken in today's world. We find Jesus Forsaken wherever toil and weariness is required of us, wherever suffering is asked of us. Like Marilen, we must always receive Him with a great "yes," and receive Him without allowing for interruptions in our love. Marilen, in her sweetness and humility, was saying that she hadn't until now made a sufficient effort in her thrust toward sanctity. She was therefore committed to do so, and her acts of charity, which she was counting on a rosary ring, would increase in number each day, an impressive number. Her whole day was a continual "for you," as if it were almost one continuous "yes."

We too, we too must do the same. Let's promise this to Jesus: I will love You from this moment on without ever stopping. I will do in one day what I would have done in three, in both the quantity and quality of my acts of charity. And if our efforts fail one day, we will begin again the next. If this will be true for us, then what had happened to Marilen in her last moments will happen also for us: her pale and drawn countenance, so consumed and in pain had come suddenly aglow, serene, relieved, and in peace. Could it be that Jesus and Mary had in some way manifested themselves to her? Had they come to take her with them?

The same will happen to us, when after having loved so much, He will manifest Himself with His great and immense love. And everything will have been completed; we will have reached sanctity.

Then we agree: during the next two weeks — to love Him without letting up.

April 3, 1986

To Follow Jesus

Throughout the Focolare this year we will go into depth on that hinge of our spirituality we call the "Word of God." It would be a good idea then, at least this one time, to stop for a moment and examine the impact that the Word has on our life. You know that a constant concern of ours is that with the passing of time the Word (or the spiritual thought of the conference call which summarizes or reminds us of it) may lose the revolutionary strength it had at the beginning of the Focolare, and for that matter, the strength that had given rise to the Focolare itself. Don't we say that the Focolare began through our living the Word, through putting the Word into practice, through keeping the Word in our hearts and in our lives?

In fact, the Focolare had not existed beforehand. But once the Gospel was put into practice, one sentence after another, a community of persons who had not previously known each other was formed, and they began to love one another; from persons scattered about, a small people was formed: the beginnings of the Focolare.

We want to ask ourselves — does the Word still have this same influence upon our lives today?

If we look at the Work of Mary in general, we can answer affirmatively. At the Focolare's periphery, or as we say, where the Focolare is on the front lines, there are numerous Word of Life groups that have the sole purpose of learning how to put the Word into practice. They are groups that we visit and to whom we communicate other aspects of our spirituality and gradually bring into contact with the entire life of the Work of Mary.

Therefore, we can really see in these groups that living the Word is the way to build the Focolare. This cannot but give us joy and a sense of gratitude to God. But for us who are already involved in the Focolare, does the Word have this dynamic, revolutionary and transforming power?

We could answer positively if we experience the effects that we know it brings and which are listed in our treatise on the Word.

As we know, the Word must change all our relationships: our relationship with God and those with our neighbors. Through the Word we should be able to discover the presence of the Father in our lives, who intervenes with His Providence, fulfills His evangelical promises to the letter, so that we might live the Word to the letter.

So then, looking at the Focolare as it appears before us, we can see that at least some of these effects are present. Doesn't the Word (or the conference call which is linked to the Word) resolve all our personal problems? Doesn't the Word bring us to live and to relive the presence of the Risen Lord within us through our repeated efforts to embrace Jesus Forsaken?

And giving us the strength to stand on our own two feet, doesn't it help us to love others, to be outside of ourselves, projected toward the service of our neighbors and toward the practice of the New Commandment? Doesn't all this bring about renewed relationships with our neighbors? Doesn't this keep the Focolare alive throughout all of its components and then cause its expansion?

In regards to God's Providence, isn't this a daily reality in many parts of the "ideal" world, just as it was during the very beginnings of the Focolare?

Yes, for as much as we can see, the Word is still carrying out its purpose. Furthermore, it appears to me that many of us have taken hold of the Word as though it were the anchor of our salvation. In general the Word is the basis of our living, of all our activity. Therefore there is reason to be joyful. The Spirit has not abandoned us, but has helped us to remain faithful to Him, and to put the *porro unum*[28] in its proper place.

---

[28]*Cf. Lk 10:41-42: "The Lord in reply said to her: 'Martha, Martha, you are anxious and upset about many things; one thing is required. Mary has chosen the better portion and she shall not be deprived of it.' "*

Of course, if we look case by case, we could always do better and more, but we cannot deny that God has helped us, that the Focolare is alive, and that the revolution brought about through the Word continues.

Now that we have verified this fact, let's take heart to move further ahead.

This month's Word of Life tells us: "My sheep hear my voice. I know them and they follow me" (Jn 10:27). With these words, Jesus wanted to tell us that those who, through the grace of God, are open to the Word and accept it, are always more instinctively in tune with His thoughts, His sentiments, and His teachings. And He knows these persons, and loves them and they consequently follow Him as His disciples.

During these next two weeks, let's try to *follow Jesus*. His voice speaks to our hearts. He will tell us at times to revive reciprocal love, or tell us to embrace the cross.

He will suggest to us to be perfect, or to improve, or to begin again... Whatever He may tell us, let's follow Him.

To follow Jesus is the watch-word that we encourage one another to live.

April 17, 1986

Mary, a Molder of Saints

I would like to speak to you this time about a topic that is very close to my heart.

It is about Mary, and our relationship with her, about our Mother who was given to us by Jesus at the culminating moment of redemption.

The month of May that begins gives us the reason to do so; it is the month of Mary, the month of flowers.

But what pushes us even more strongly to do so is that we are the Work of Mary, that Mary is the Queen of the Focolare, our true president; and that she, as we have always said, is the model or the form of what we should become.

During these last few days I have been reading passages on Mary by various authors, most of them saints. Through these readings I am coming to realize more and more the importance of Mary in the spiritual life of a Christian who orients his or her life toward sanctity.

In fact, these authors say that Our Lady is the *"molder of saints,"* that Mary is at the center of the supernatural experiences of all who are similar to Jesus, which would be the saints; they have all been formed by Mary.[29]

Therefore, in order to become saints—and this is what we aim for through our conference calls—we must put Mary always more into her rightful place in our spiritual life. At times, as we know, the road is not easy. We encounter trials, difficulties, and obstacles that threaten to block out our good resolutions.

We can therefore understand the importance of a great union with Mary.

---

[29] *Cf.* B. Socche, Maria Mediatrice, *Reggio Emilia, 1961, p. 32.*

These authors tell us that on the way of Mary, we make progress more peacefully and more gently. Of course, even on her way there are harsh struggles to overcome; but Mary, as a good Mother, comes very close and stays by the side of her faithful in order to cast light on their darkness, to assure them in their fears, to sustain them in their battles to such an extent that it is true that this way, (the way of Mary) compared to other ways, is a way of roses and honey.[30]

Our own spiritual way is also called the "Way of Mary," *Via Mariae*.

Then let's revive our faith that Mary is near, but let's first of all renew our resolution to be very close to her. If it may appear to us that we are traveling too slowly along this way, then let's recall what the saints have affirmed: further advancement can be made in a shorter period of time through submission to and dependence on Mary (we must depend on her because she is our leader) than in entire years through our own will and self-dependency, because persons who are obedient and submissive to Mary will sing victory over all their enemies.[31]

If we see that we have already taken some steps on the way of Mary, and if it appears to us that we have with the grace of God traveled a portion of the journey, then let's trust that united with her, we will reach our goal.

It is the conviction of the saints that when the Holy Spirit, the Spouse of Mary, finds her present in a person's soul, He will enter fully and communicate to it as abundantly as the person makes room within the soul for His Spouse.[32]

Therefore, we must do everything we can to be in deep union with Mary beginning now in this month of May.

The saints, who are always so totalitarian, invite us to give all of ourselves to her, without measure, in order to be in some way, as they say (a concept that is also dear to us) "she herself

---

[30] *Cf.* L. M. Grignion de Monfort, Trattato della vera devozione alla Santa Vergine e il segreto di Maria, *Alba, 1985, p. 109, n. 152.*
[31] *Ibid., p. 111, n. 155.*
[32] *Ibid., p. 38, n. 36.*

who lives, speaks, and works within this world" through us.[33]

To be then, completely hers by giving our life to her, but also our every action and our efforts toward reaching sanctity.

To be completely hers, by offering her the *Hail Marys* of the rosary recited wholeheartedly, asking her to take special care of us and of the Work of Mary.

To be completely hers by visiting her more often in the churches and places where she is most venerated.

It is striking what the saints can invent in order to declare to her their love!

Now it is our turn!

If we are the Work of Mary, we must do as they did; we must aim at being among those in the Church who love her the most.

A proposal which would be in tune with our vocation would truly be to aim at loving her as no one else has loved her before. Imagine how much Jesus loved her. We need to have His heart to love His and our Mother. Yes, no one must surpass us in loving her, in venerating her, in praising and in singing to her. May this be our proposal: *that no one surpass us in loving Mary.*

May 1, 1986

---

[33]*Cf.* Gli Scritti di Massimiliano Kolbe, eroe di Oswiecim e beato della Chiesa, Vol. I, *Florence, 1975, p. 896.*

To Love without Holding Back

The first two weeks of May have already gone by and I am sure that we have at least begun to make an effort to increase the love that lies in our hearts for Mary.

We have done so if for no other reason than to obtain the great advantages that traveling along her way brings: those who go to Jesus through Mary — we saw this last time — find the road to sanctity much smoother, travel more swiftly, and reach the goal.

During these past few days I'm sure that many of you have declared yourselves hers, all hers, in order to become closer to Jesus.

Yes, you must have done this. A small occurrence gives us a sign of this, at least it is the way we would like to interpret it, being convinced that Our Lady does not allow herself to be outdone in generosity.

Didn't we say that we all wanted to belong to her?

Mary answered us, and in some way told us the she is ours. She said so through the words of our Holy Father John Paul II who has almost coined for us (and nothing happens by chance) a new litany.

We were in the last hour of our Congress which dealt with the community life of the parish and all the participants were at St. Peter's Square to recite the prayer *Regina Coeli* (Queen of Heaven) with the Pope.

The Pontiff, after having called to mind the Easter celebration of the Orthodox Church, and after having addressed very beautiful words to us as well, had added:

"Once again I greet all of you present, thankful for this communion of prayer... in which all of us offer Easter wishes to the Mother of the Risen Christ; ...to our Mother, our Mother Mary; *Mary of the Focolarini, (Mary) of the Focolare...* "

What jubilation for our hearts! This struck us so much that we decided to give this name to the beautiful sculptural relief on Mary, which a married Focolarino is preparing for the Mariapolis Center of Castelgandolfo: "St. Mary of the Focolarini."

"Mary of the Focolarini." Yes, it is very probable that Mary wanted to declare herself "ours" through the Holy Father. Doesn't the Word of Life "Give, and it shall be given to you" (Lk 6:38) always hold true?

We gave ourselves to her and she gave herself to us.

Therefore, we are very grateful to Mary for this and we would like to think that this comes as a new grace from her.

So then, in a competition of love let's continue to love Mary with growing intensity.

We can do this by traveling swiftly along her way, the *Way of Mary* which is our way.

This way of hers contemplates all the steps of her life and our entire spirituality which draws us to travel this road.

Among other things, it is a contemplation of living the Word in a radical way.

This month's Word of Life tells us: "But you are not in the flesh; you are in the spirit, since the Spirit of God dwells in you" (Rom 8:9).

Yes, the Spirit of God dwells in us.

And we know what the Spirit of God produces within us.

He infuses love into our hearts.

Let's allow ourselves to burn and be ablaze with this love.

That it may consume everything within us! Without sparing a thing!

That nothing in us be kept from burning to ashes.

In short, let's love God with all of our hearts. And to do this well, let's love our neighbors with all of our heart, mind and strength.

Jesus did not spare anything of Himself in loving us: He gave His life for us.

Mary did not even spare her Son for us: she needed to lose Him not only because He was dying, but because Jesus, in a certain way, entrusting her to John, was relieving her from her task of being His Mother.

We need to lose everything out of love for others. Our love

must have this kind of measure.

Let's examine all the opportunities that we have during the day to love, beginning with our neighbors who are closest to us, those with whom we work, those for whom our apostolate within the Work of Mary must serve, and let's see if we are in the disposition to give of ourselves entirely: our strength, will and intelligence.

Our interior voice knows how to give us the answer. And if the response is positive, let's be at peace. If otherwise, then let's correct our actions and love without holding anything back.

In doing so, we will reset our revolution of love in motion.

This is what Mary, in interpreting the plan of God for us, wants for us.

Therefore let's be decisive: in order to love Mary and to live her commands, let's love our neighbors all the way to the end, without holding back.

May 15, 1986

Choose Jesus Forsaken in order to be Fit for the Kingdom of God

This splendid month of May has now gone by. During the month, throughout the Focolare we have tried to increase our love for our Heavenly Mother.

I too, as I think you have, wanted to do my part to show my devotion to Mary, also by taking concrete measures. For this reason I went to visit her where she is most venerated: at her shrines. In Rome I visited the shrine of Mentorella and of Divine Love. In Florence, the shrine of Monte Senario of the Seven Founding Saints and in Trent, the shrine of Baselga di Pine and Our Lady of Laste.

At each visit I entrusted all of you to Mary. And each time, I experienced a consolation to the point of sensing a peculiar desire: that we too might possess a shrine, and erect a church entirely in her honor.

When I was at Loppiano, I imagined this shrine to be situated inside our little city.

But then an answer came from within, perhaps from Mary herself: "I don't want a shrine of stone from all of you. I want all of *you*. You are all living stones of my shrine. Don't you say that you journey along the "Way of Mary" in order to become another me? Are you not the stones which along the Holy Journey the Holy Spirit smoothens, making them perfect and fitting for a construction of this kind?

Then I understood: Loppiano—and our other permanent Mariapolises as well—is not only—as we have defined it—a city-school whose teacher is Jesus in our midst, nor only a city on the hilltop, and not even just a city where the Gospel is lived.

Loppiano can be considered a city-Mary, where the citizens try to live like Mary, whether it be as individuals or as a collectivity, therefore where Mary in a certain way relives mystically in them.

Loppiano can be seen as a city whose atmosphere is lightened by the spirit of Mary, which can be experienced by the thousands of its visitors in a way similar to being at the Marian shrines.

I shared these thoughts of mine to the citizens of Loppiano and this gave them great joy and the desire to make a deeper commitment.

Then, thinking about it for a moment, I understood that the entire Work of Mary, spread throughout the world as it is, can be considered a Marian shrine.

Isn't the Focolare a vast Mariapolis in the world? Isn't it true that we all want to become another little Mary, both singularly and all together?

Yes, we are all an edifice built in her honor; we are, or better we must be, a concrete form of praise raised from all the earth to Mary.

Therefore, let's revive this awareness within ourselves and live with this thought in mind, this treasure in our hearts, and then we will not have the nostalgia to see that the month of May has passed us by, but instead we will be able to extend the month of May to the length of the entire year. We will remain with Mary throughout all twelve months and she will remain with us to teach us how to love Jesus, to comfort us in our sorrows, to guide us along her path, to bring us to sanctity.

And so that this may be lived concretely, let's see which Word of Life will serve to enlighten our way during these next two weeks. It reads: "Whoever puts his hand to the plow but keeps looking back is unfit for the reign of God" (Lk 9:62).

"Keeps looking back." What does this looking back mean? It means to go back to our former ways, to take back into consideration and live for our previous ideals.

With this Word of Life Jesus warns those who put their hands to the plow, meaning those who have made good resolutions, not to turn back because it will render them incapable of bringing forward the Kingdom of God.

At a certain point of our lives, we have chosen Jesus Forsaken as the everything of our lives. We chose Him as our preference over all other things.

This commits us to remain faithful to Him.

To choose Jesus Forsaken above all else means to love suffering and the effort required to live the virtues more than joys, consolations and the gifts of God. It means to love those neighbors in whose countenance we discover Him more than all our other neighbors.

It means to love the goals of the Work of Mary: unity with the Catholics with whom our unity of love is not yet perfect, unity with our brothers and sisters of other Churches, the faithful of other religions, and those who are far from God.

Now, in order to be fit for His Kingdom, meaning the Work of Mary, we must hold firm to the totality of this love.

This is what we must reconfirm for ourselves during the next two weeks—to say to Jesus Forsaken: "You are the one I want, my love has no other choice. I live for you. You are the meaning of my life."

If we do so, we will journey along the "Way of Mary" without stopping. Mary will superimpose her own image upon us; we will be new creatures as she is because the Risen Lord will live within us, and thus we will contribute toward making the Work of Mary a shrine of hers.

Let's remember then: "Choose Jesus Forsaken in order to be fit for the Kingdom of God."

June 5, 1986

Look at Jesus Forsaken and You Will Find the Answer

We are united once again to strongly inspire one another to walk, or better still, to run along the way of sanctity.

In fact, the Word of Life of this month tells us: "...persevere in running the race which lies ahead; let us keep our eyes fixed on Jesus..." (Heb 12:1-2).

The road of life is often like an obstacle course. There are trials, and there are many kinds of sufferings. This is why we must keep our eyes fixed on Jesus, furthermore, on Jesus Forsaken.

This time I would like to address a word above all to those—some of whom I am aware—who are undergoing spiritual or physical trials, and tell them: "Look at Jesus Forsaken and you will find the answer."

In fact, Jesus Forsaken is the model for overcoming trials.

An aspect of Jesus Forsaken, and perhaps one of the most painful is, after having allowed one's whole spiritual life to be permeated by faith in the love of God, a person, through various circumstances feels abandoned by Him.

Even in this situation, one must look at Jesus Forsaken. Didn't Jesus say that everyone would abandon Him except the Father who would always be with Him?[34]

However, in His abandonment the opposite holds true. The Father seems to have forsaken Him. It is a terrible, tragic moment. And what does He do? He let's out a loud cry, but then He reabandons Himself to the Father.

In these circumstances, we must do the same. These are moments, I think, that have great value in front of God.

---

[34] *Cf. Jn 16:32:* "*An hour is coming—has indeed already come—when you will be scattered and each will go his way, leaving me quite alone. (Yet I can never be alone; the Father is with me.)*

In His abandonment Jesus completed the redemption.

In our own, united to His, we cooperate in our own purification and who knows how many souls we will help in the process.

Jesus Forsaken is truly the solution to every problem. In Him we will never find delusion, but rather the explanation of all our trials.

So then, take heart! Let's keep our eyes fixed on Him in order to overcome every obstacle along our way.

August 14, 1986

Call Him by Name

We are still in the month in which the Word of Life (Heb 12:1) invites us to transform our lives into a race, keeping our eyes on Jesus, and in particular as we have added, on Jesus Forsaken.

Last time we saw how life can be considered an obstacle course.

But what are these obstacles? How can they be defined?

It is always a great discovery to see how we can in a certain way give the name Jesus Forsaken to every suffering and trial of life.

Have we been taken by fear? Hadn't Jesus on the cross in His abandonment appeared to be overcome with the fear that the Father may have forgotten Him?

The obstacle that we can find in certain harsh trials is discouragement. In His abandonment Jesus seems to be immersed in the impression that in His divine passion He lacks the Father's comfort and appears to be losing the courage to complete His utmost trial, but then adds, "Father, into your hands I commend my spirit" (Lk 23:46).

Do circumstances cause us to feel disoriented? In His tremendous suffering, Jesus appears to not understand what is happening to Him as He crys "Why?" (cf. Mt 27:46; Mk 15:34).

Do we face opposition? In His abandonment, hadn't the Father seemed to disapprove of what the Son had done?

Have we been reprimanded, or been faced with accusations?

On the cross, Jesus in His abandonment perhaps had the impression of being reprimanded, or faced with an accusation even from Heaven.

And then in certain trials in life that can follow one after another, don't we even reach the point of saying that it seems too much, or beyond measure? In His abandonment Jesus drank from a bitter chalice that was not only full, but overflowing. His trial was one that was beyond measure.

And when we are surprised by delusion, or wounded by a trauma, or by an unforeseen misfortune, or by a sickness or an absurd situation, we can always recall the suffering of Jesus Forsaken who impersonated all these trials and thousands of others.

Yes, He is present in everything that can cause suffering. Each suffering is another name for Him.

There is an expression used in the world that says that you call the one you love by name.

We have decided to love Jesus Forsaken.

And then, to better succeed in doing so, let's get used to calling Him by name in the various trials of our life.

We will call Him: Jesus Forsaken-loneliness, Jesus Forsaken-doubt, Jesus Forsaken-hurt, Jesus Forsaken-trial, Jesus Forsaken-desolation and so forth.

And calling Him by name, He will see that He is discovered and recognized under every suffering, and will respond to us with more love; by embracing Him He will become our peace, our comfort, courage, stability, our health and our victory. He will be the explanation and the solution to everything.

Let's try then during the next two weeks to call by name that Jesus that we encounter in the obstacles of life. We will overcome them more swiftly and our lives' courses will not experience any delays.

August 28, 1986

Giving Joy to Heaven

The Word of Life for the month of September speaks about joy. It tells us: "I tell you there will be the same kind of joy before the angels of Heaven over one repentant sinner" (Lk 15:10).

Joy in Heaven! A new joy added to the joy that already fills Heaven. And why? For one single sinner that converts.

How important conversions are for Heaven!

At this point it becomes spontaneous for us to think about the Work of Mary.

We have said it many times: the activities of the Focolare are not primarily the concrete projects expressing the various works of mercy. The typical task of the Work of Mary is not found in building institutes to house orphans, or the aged, or the drug addicted, the handicapped, the sick or the dying... as numerous religious families and associations of the Church do and ourselves as well, particularly through the Youth for a United World and the New Humanity Movements.

The works of the Work of Mary are principally conversions.

The numerous returns to God that take place throughout the world where the Focolare is spread are our characteristic works, our fruits.

We gather them in our various meetings, Mariapolises, through the very life of unity in the focolare centers, the nucleuses of Volunteers, the Gen units, the permanent Mariapolises... They come about through our printed works and through our various means of communication.

If these conversions have always been a cause for our joy, then in this month in which the Word of Life tells us of the same effect given to Heaven through just one single conversion, our heart's joy cannot but also be increased.

Perhaps we have not given much thought about this fact, but it would be good to do so often during this month.

Keeping this in mind will encourage us to work for the Work of Mary in all of its sectors, in all of its manifestations with a renewed zeal and with greater commitment and perfection.

Just think: one single conversion down here brings joy up there! What would be the result of the so many conversions brought about by Jesus in our midst?

The Word of Life of this month cannot but give us the conviction of heart that Jesus and Mary and all of Heaven rejoice precisely for this purpose that the Focolare has, for the fruits that it gathers, for all that we do.

We have certainly experienced that the better we work in the Work of Mary and the more we pray and offer our sufferings out of love for her, the more abundant are the fruits we gather.

So then it will be easy to draw a conclusion from today's thought: let's live in such a way that Heaven may experience the greatest added joy for the many sinners that return.

We will reach this objective by dedicating ourselves in the course of these next two weeks particularly to those we know personally and by giving generously our own contribution to the activities in the Work of Mary we are committed to.

Therefore, our motto will be: "Let's work perfectly for the Work of Mary in order to give joy to Heaven."

September 11, 1986

Spending the Day with Mary

Last time we hoped to encourage one another to dedicate ourselves to the Work of Mary with the greatest possible commitment and perfection.

Now that we are at the close of the month of September, in which we have celebrated two special feasts of Mary, today we would want above all to see how we can renew our personal rapport with her, the Focolare's leader. We want to examine the daily contacts we have with her, and to see how well we show our love to her: practically speaking, to see what our day with her should be like.

As many of us already do, a good thing as soon as we rise in the morning, after having focused in on the reason for which we live by saying, "Because you are forsaken..." we should add: "Because you are desolate, Mary," as if to say that our life should not be lived only out of love for Jesus Forsaken but also in union with Mary Desolate; my life should be such that the passion and death of Jesus and the great sorrow of Mary suffered at the foot of the cross for humanity, should not go lost, but be given their greatest value.

As we know, we have various possibilities of being with Mary. A particular thought of ours is addressed to her during morning and evening prayer. We remember Mary at mass and during the visit to the Blessed Sacrament, and above all during the recitation of the rosary, in which we greet her more than fifty times with the *"Hail Mary."*

Each phrase of the *Hail Mary* is beautiful, but today I would suggest to underline in a special way during the next two weeks this double request: "Pray for us sinners *now* and *at the hour of our death,*" so that Mary may assist us by interceding for us before God in each present moment and so that in the important moment of death she may be present to us in a special way.

But if all these prayers prove to be important for us during our day, what I would want to particularly bring to surface today is the relationship that we must have with Mary. It is a relationship that must be kept alive during the whole course of the day and will grow in depth in accordance with the degree of unity that each of us reaches with her, our most amiable Mother and leader.

First of all, as members of the Work of Mary we can reflect that, if we do belong to the Focolare, it is not only because God has chosen us, but also Mary along with Him. We, each one of us, have certainly one day been looked upon with a special love of hers and brought here.

Then we can also imagine that she has lead us to the Focolare, because since she loved us she wanted to also show herself in a special way to us as our Mother.

Now what does a mother do for her children.

We know: she does everything without calculating her efforts.

Then, if this is true for an earthly mother, what will our Heavenly Mother be like?

We must become convinced of her very special love for us and then draw a conclusion from this. Does Mary love me? More so, does she love me in a special way? I cannot but have a boundless trust in her who can do so much. Therefore I will entrust to her everything that is mine, not only my own self, but my thoughts and my worries, what weighs me down, what hurts me. Mary wants all these things for herself and she is very capable of resolving every problem of mine.

I tell you these things beause I experienced that if we take her love for us seriously, our Mother will not neglect to show this love to us.

Try to do the same. Perhaps you have already done so.

Try not to keep any burden in your heart, and to entrust everything to her. You will find one problem resolved after another.

Finally, I would like us to introduce a beautiful practice into our life of unity with Mary.

You know how we keep the presence of Jesus among us alive by declaring to one another, "Let's keep Jesus in our midst." Now why can't we do this also with Mary? This would mean that we must be ready to die for her as she did for us. It would mean to be ready to die for her mystically present in the Work of Mary.

Who knows how happy Mary would be to have the possibility of giving new life to Jesus together with us, even though only spiritually.

I have experienced how beautiful and marvelous it is to close my eyes in the evening after having said to her, "Let's keep Jesus in our midst."

So these are just a few words on spending our day with Mary.

That she may allow us to experience her motherly affection and guard us as the pupils of her eyes.

During the next two weeks then, let's revive our unity with Mary.

September 25, 1986

The Lifestyle of the Work of Mary is Love

Lately we have seen how Heaven loves and rejoices over conversions. Consequently, we have made the commitment to work with perfection within the Work of Mary, which brings these kinds of fruits. First of all, we have tried during these last two weeks to perfect our relationship with the one who is the leader and primary foundress of the Focolare: Mary.

Let's see today what style our actions within the Work of Mary should assume.

A new Ideal year is beginning for us, and in order to diligently accomplish all that is expected of us, we must be well equipped with virtue. St. Paul, in the Word of Life of this month, invites us to not be timid in our service to God, but to be strong, and full of love and wisdom.[35] Now where do we need to look in order to acquire and develop these and other virtues which we need?

It is easy, and our ideal has the answer: allow Jesus to live within us in the place of our own ego.

But how can Jesus live in us? By being love as God is Love. (cf. 1 Jn 4:16). Therefore, we must go out of ourselves in order to love the others.

We always speak of love and it could seem superfluous to underline it again this time. But this is not so. The "old man" (cf. Ef 4:22) — the absence of love — is always ready to take the upperhand in us, hidden behind thousands of excuses. This new year which we are beginning must decisively see the "new man" resplendent (cf. Ef 4:24) in each of us. Therefore we will work well where we are; we will move ahead and build the Work of Mary, and through it, the Church.

---

[35] *"The Spirit God has given us is no cowardly spirit, but rather one that makes us strong, loving and wise" (2 Tim 1:7).*

Let's go back then to the alpha of our spirituality: love. Besides, this is what our charism is. This is what the world is most in need of today.

Let's look around us. Where do we find the love which Jesus brought to earth?

People pass by one another everywhere, in the streets, the stores, the coffee shops, in offices, but they are indifferent toward one another. We read the newspapers: their headlines almost always speak of sad happenings, of violence. There is still human love that keeps many families and friendships together, but it is difficult to find Christian love. We can discover it in various Christian oases as among consecrated persons or communities of dedicated Christians. In general, however, it is not found in today's world.

And we have been raised up and chosen by God together with others precisely in order to bring this love. It is our gift, our great gift which we must give to humanity.

It is true: we are many, but we are also very few in comparison with the population of the world. And God has spread us out everywhere, and since we are so spread out, we can rarely give a large scale global witness as to what the nature of Christianity truly is, what its love really is.

But let's not lose heart.

If God through us has laid out a net across the entire earth, the time will come when it will get increasingly tighter and the world will have a better means, also through our own work, to recognize the fire that Jesus has brought to earth.

This will be a reality tomorrow if today we are what we should be. We must be love, exactly what the world is not.

Love is the lifestyle of the Work of Mary.

Let's go out of ourselves, therefore, and love! And let's keep on this direction. Let's begin very decidedly. Let's set the Work of Mary in motion: let's rekindle love in our hearts.

So that the world may soon find true love everywhere, let's commit ourselves fully to love everyone!

October 9, 1986

Live the Present to Perfection

One of the major occurences of these last two weeks has been Lionello's[36] sudden and unexpected departure for the Heavenly Mariapolis. Lionello was one of the most mature and learned Focolarini of the Work of Mary; a Focolarino to whom the Work of Mary owes much for the example of his transparent life, so supernatural and detached from the things of this world, completely given to the service of God and his neighbors.

His departure was sudden and unexpected not only for us, but for he himself, which calls to our attention other departures that were so different in nature because they were prepared for at length, like the death of Luminosa, Margrit, and Marilen. Therefore, there are those among us who complete their Holy Journey after waiting for a long time, and there are those who complete it as if in a flash of lightning, when it is least expected.

This makes us ask ourselves: What will it be like for us? Our instinctive reaction is to draw the conclusion: it is good to be always prepared. How? Remaining in the grace of God and living the present moment fully.

Lionello's swift departure gave me the desire in these last few days to keep fixing my attention on that typical aspect of our spirituality which consists in concentrating on living the present moment. My mind took me back to the many phrases I had gathered from the saints who encourage us to put this into practice with perfection.

Do you recall any of them?

---

[36] *Lionello Bonfanti, a former public prosecutor of the city of Parma, Italy, has been associated with the Focolare since 1953. A priest Focolarino, he was part of the body of directors of the Work of Mary.*

St. Catherine of Siena said: "We do not possess the toil of the past, because that time has escaped us; nor the toil that is to come, because we cannot be certain to have that time."[37] By saying this, she extends an invitation to live the present.

And St. Teresa of Lisieux: "You know, my God, that to love You...I only have today."[38]

Then I remembered a motto that was so useful to us in the past and which we remembered very easily because each word in Italian began with an "s": *Sarò santa se sono santa subito.* (I will become a saint if I am a saint right now.)

I have noticed in these last few days how this way of living life was dear to other saints who fervently advise it.

St. Paul of the Cross wrote: "Fortunate is the soul who rests in God, without thinking of the future, but tries to live moment by moment in God, without any other desire than to do the will of God well in every situation..."[39]

"Fortunate is the soul... "

We can make this fortune our own, because it is within our spirituality to live in this way.

It is by living the present moment that we can fulfill all our responsibilities.

It is by living the present moment that our crosses become bearable: it is not without purpose that this practice is advised for those who are aware of their approaching death.

It is by living the present moment that we can seize the inspirations of God, the impulses of His grace that come to us in the present moment.

It is by living the present moment that we can fruitfully build our sanctity. St. Frances de Sales said: "Each moment carries a particular command which sinks back into eternity recording what we have done with it."

Therefore, let's live the present moment.

It has been a while since we have underlined this duty of ours. Let's thank Lionello for having reminded us of this with his departure.

---

[37] *St. Catherine of Siena,* Epistolario, *cit., II, p. 97.*
[38] *St. Teresa of the Child Jesus,* Gli Scritti, *Rome, 1970, p. 818.*
[39] *St. Paul of the Cross,* Lettere, I, *Rome, 1924, pp. 645-646.*

Let's live the present moment to perfection!

We will find ourselves at the evening of each day and at the evening of life, rich in good works accomplished and in acts of charity offered.

Let's remember: live the present moment to perfection.

October 23, 1986

Renewing Reciprocal Love

Those responsible for all the different zones have now ended their meetings and have returned to their countries to be with you again.

Their first task—and I know that in some zones this is already being carried out—will be to inform you about everything that has been seen here at our headquarters: programs, updatings, developments, directives.... They will also have to share with you about the different events we lived through together, including Lionello's passage to the Heavenly Mariapolis.

With what kind of attitude should you listen to these things so that they might be fruitful for you?

It is evident; you must prepare the good soil within your own souls and in the various communities.

How? By making the effort once again to live the Ideal, our spirituality, in its fullness.

The Word of Life for November is so helpful for us to do so. It says: "Let us cast off deeds of darkness and put on the armor of light" (Rom 13:12).

The "deeds of darkness" are the consequences of vices and sin. The "armor of light" is the virtues and the practice of living the Word of God in our lives.

Now, we know that the New Commandment of Jesus is the synthesis of all His commands, of all His Words.

Therefore, we will put on the "armor of light" by refocusing our lives on this commandment.

The result—we know—is that the Risen Lord will be resplendent in the midst of our community, and there would be no better ground than His presence to receive what will be offered to you: with His presence among you, everything will be received with an open heart.

Certainly, the one who has done the most work, also

among those responsible for the zones gathered here at Rocca di Papa for the month of October, has been Jesus in our midst. And now it is His fire and His light that are being brought into the zones.

However, if this fire encounters another fire, if this light encounters another light, the Work of Mary in the various zones will be able to truly hope to achieve the development that God has planned for it during this ideal year that we are beginning.

So then, the "armor of light." The New Commandment practiced with new commitment. The result will be that this new year which we are preparing to live will be an authentic year of living our Holy Journey.

Here at our headquarters, before beginning to work, we decided amongst ourselves to live the 1986-87 year as the most holy year of our lives. And so that this may come true, we decided to always be the living message of the conference call.

This is an invitation which I extend to all of you.

And so that we can begin right away, let's take a moment to look at our reciprocal love: let's consider the measure of love (keeping in mind that it must be the same measure of Jesus toward us: therefore to be ready to give our lives), let's look at where our generosity is lacking, at our limitations in loving, so that we can overcome them; let's see if our reciprocal love may rest too heavily on a human plane, and need therefore to be raised to a supernatural level....

If we do so, if we improve our reciprocal love in this way, Jesus, the Saint, will be among us and will make this present year the holiest of our lives.

Reciprocal love, therefore, renewed in its fullness in order to receive the updatings well, in order to live the Word of Life, in order to become saints.

This is our commitment for the next two weeks.

October 23, 1986

The Necessary Attributes for Those who Want to Undertake a Holy Journey

We continue our journey, whose end we hope, if God helps us, will be crowned in sanctity.

Several among those who have undertaken this journey have arrived, and for as much as we can know, they have done so successfully. Every week we receive news concerning such arrivals and very often we see how God must truly be praised.

The greater number of us are still here on earth to inspire one another: this is the purpose of our conference call.

Its purpose is to transform our life into a Holy Journey, to produce the result desired in the *Imitation of Christ,* a book of prayer and meditation so rich in spirituality which many of us are familiar with, which says that we need some attributes that are very compelling: complete contempt for the world, an ardent desire to progress in virtue, love for sacrifice, the fervor of penance, self-denial, and knowing how to bear every adversity....

They are attributes that are necessary for all of us to possess. However, we must ask ourselves: how can we acquire them in accordance with our own spirituality?

The answer is clear and certain: we have not been called by God to accomplish all this through a monastic style of life separated from the world. We are called to remain in the midst of the world and to arrive at God through our neighbor, which means through love for our neighbor and through reciprocal love.

It is through committing ourselves to undertake this unique and evangelical path that we will discover, as if by enchantment, that we have acquired these virtues in our soul.

We need to have contempt for the world.

There is no better contempt for something than complete disregard, forgetfullness and indifference toward its existence.

If we are all projected toward thinking of the others, toward loving the others, we no longer have concern for the world, we forget about it; therefore, we have contempt for it, even though this does not free us from doing our part in pushing aside its suggestions when they assail us.

We must progress in virtue. But we can do this if we have love. Isn't it written: "I will run the way of your commands when you give me a docile heart [a heart full of love]" (Psalm 119:32).

If in loving our neighbor we run the path of fulfilling God's commands, it means that we are making progress.

We need love for sacrifice.

To love the others precisely means to sacrifice oneself in order to be dedicated to the service of others. Christian love, even though it is a source of great joy, is synonomous with sacrifice.

We need the fervor of penance. It is through a life of love that we will find the greatest and principal penance to perform.

We need self-denial.

Love for our neighbors always implies self-denial.

Finally, we need to know how to bear all adversity.

Are not many sufferings in the world caused by living alongside of others?

We must know how to bear everyone, and to love them out of love for Jesus Forsaken. By doing this we will overcome many obstacles in life.

Yes, in loving our neighbor we find an excellent possibility to transform our life into a Holy Journey.

Let's commit ourselves then to living this love of ours in a totalitarian, radical and fully tolerant way, exercising all our energy in doing so; let's resolve to render our love concrete, as a true service, so that when we examine ourselves we will be able to say: yes, out of love I have forgotten the world, I have progressed in the virtues, I have sacrificed myself, I have done penance, and I have lived self-denial.

During these next two weeks, let's continue to place love for our neighbor and reciprocal love at the center of our lives.

It will be the best way to prepare for Advent, the season of the year in which we await the coming of the Lord.

With this love, Jesus will be reborn in us, and among us, and what could be a better way to prepare for Christmas?

November 11, 1986

Who is the Layperson for the Church?

The 1986-87 year is an important one for the Catholic world. In fact, preparations are being made to celebrate the Synod of Bishops which will be held in the fall, concerning the "Vocation and mission of the laity in the Church and in the world twenty years after the Second Vatican Council."

It is an important year for the Catholic laity, but also — I think — for other Christians in whose Churches the role of the laity is often stressed.

We too, who desire to be committed Christians, are preparing for this Synod through prayer, which must never be lacking, and through the work which is asked of us.

But, "Who is the layperson?" This is a reoccurring question in the Church today. How can the layperson be identified or defined? Many people are trying to give the answer. In fact, no one would really want to define the layperson in terms that show what the lay person is not: a person who is neither a priest, nor a religious. Instead, one would want to establish who the layperson *is*.

For this reason we would like to offer a contribution to the study of this topic, by affirming what someone might call Columbus's egg: the layperson is a Christian. As such, laypersons are followers of Christ and His Gospel. For this reason they must fully live what Jesus wants from them, and to work first of all toward enhancing the Kingdom of God, toward building the Church. Given that they have the possibility of being in the midst of the world, it is there where they will bring the light of the Gospel, passing its effect onto all things.

This is who the layperson is for us — a well formed follower of Christ, who has the two-fold task of building the Church and to Christianize the world.

We laypersons of the Focolare find ourselves reflected very well in this image of a layperson. In fact, the Focolare has on one side a spiritual aspect, if we can use the expression, where we work in order that Christ might grow in us and among us, and therefore build the Church; and then an aspect that is more human and concrete, where we work toward permeating the various sectors of society with the spirit of Christ.

We strongly identify ourselves with this type of layperson, and because of this we feel we are finely tuned to what the Second Vatican Council has defined in this regard.

We identify ourselves with this definition and we would like this year to always improve in living our specific vocation as laypersons so that we too can give our contribution to the Synod.

Therefore, how should we live these next two weeks?

Let's try to be true laypersons of the Church, meaning authentic followers of Christ, who live His words and what the rest of Sacred Scripture proposes.

We have a splendid Word of Life for this month which underlines what we lived last month on reciprocal love. It tells us: "Accept one another, then, as Christ accepted you, for the glory of God" (Rm 15:7). In putting into practice this Word of Life among us, we will maintain firm the basis upon which the Work of Mary, which is Church, is built.

In putting this Word into practice with other Christians, in places where we can find ourselves working within ecclesial structures, we will still give our specific contribution to the development of the Church.

Living these words in the world of the family and in the various sectors of society, we will place the most important basis for being able to attain the Christian renewal of laws and structures.

This conference call — as you have noticed — serves in a special way for laypersons.

But the Word of Life is for everyone: laypersons, priests and religious. Let's put it into practice in all our respective fields of service.

Let's accept each neighbor as Christ has accepted us.

He has accepted us, and accepts us each day and each hour we call upon Him. Whoever we are, sinners or saints, young or old, beautiful or ugly, healthy or sickly, He always accepts all of us. And we are so sure of His acceptance, of His forgiveness, and of His hospitality, that it doesn't even pass our minds for a moment that it could be otherwise. Let's act accordingly in regard to our neighbors. That they may always find us with open hearts, always available for them, always ready to receive them.

Let's live in this way. And may it be for the glory of God.

December 11, 1986

Christmas with Those who Suffer

It is Christmas day and our conference call could not have fallen on a better date.

In fact, this gives us the chance to exchange our wishes in person.

Wishes for what?

It is logical: wishes for a Holy Journey lived together in this year 1986-87, which we want to be the holiest year of our lives.

Best wishes to everyone, but very special ones to a particular group of persons.

Today the warmth of Christmas brings all of us to feel more as a family, more one among us, more brothers and sisters: to want to share therefore, in everything: joys and sorrows.

We want to share the sorrows above all with those who, through various circumstances, are spending this Christmas in direct contact with suffering.

This is the group of persons for whom we would like to address this conference call in a particular way.

Suffering!

The suffering which at times strikes our entire beings and the suffering which arises and mixes together the bitter and pleasant moments of our day.

Suffering: a sickness, a misfortune, a trial, a painful circumstance...

Suffering!

How should we look upon its occurrence, which is very present in this period of time for many members of the Focolare, or look upon the suffering which is always ready to appear in each one's life?

How can it be defined? Be identified? What name can it be called by? Whose voice is it?

If we look at suffering from a human standpoint, we are tempted to look for its cause either within us or outside of us, for example, in human malice, or in nature or other things.... That accident is Steven's fault; that sickness is my fault; that painful trial came about because of Richard....

And all this can still be true, but if we think only in these terms, we forget something more important. We lose sight of the fact that behind the sequence of our lives lies the love of God who wills or permits everything for a higher purpose, which is our own good.

For this reason, the saints take every painful circumstance they encounter right from the hands of God. It is striking how they never go wrong in this regard.

For them, suffering is the voice of God, and nothing else.

Immersed as they are in the Sacred Scriptures, they understand what suffering is and what it must be for a Christian; they grasp the transformation that Jesus had worked, seeing how He had changed it from a negative element to a positive one.

The explanation of their suffering is Jesus Himself: Jesus crucified.

For this reason suffering becomes even something that can be loved, it becomes something good.

For this reason they do not curse suffering, but bear, accept and embrace it.

If we open the New Testament ourselves, we will find this attitude confirmed.

Doesn't St. James say in his letter, "My brothers, count it pure joy when you are involved in every sort of trial (Jm 1:2)?

Suffering therefore, is even a cause for joy.

After having invited us to take up our cross and follow Him, doesn't Jesus then affirm, "He who seeks only himself brings himself to ruin, whereas he who brings himself to naught [and this is the apex of suffering] discovers who he is" (Mt 10:39)?

Suffering therefore is hope of salvation.

For St. Paul, suffering is even something to boast of, more so, the only thing to boast of: "May I never boast of anything but the cross of our Lord Jesus Christ" (Gal 6:14).

Yes, for those who consider it from a Christian viewpoint, suffering is a great thing: it even gives us the chance to complete in ourselves the passion of Christ for our own purification and for the redemption of many.

So then, what can we say to those who are struggling with suffering? What wish can we offer them? How can we relate to them?

First of all, let's approach them with the greatest respect: even though they may not think so, in this moment they are being visited by God.

Then, in every way possible, let's share their crosses, and therefore truly keep Jesus in the midst with them. Let's assure them that we are continually with them, and assure them of our prayers, so that they may know how to take what distresses and causes them to suffer directly from the hands of God, and unite it to Jesus' passion so that it can produce its greatest fruit.

Let's help them to always have the value of suffering present before them.

And let's remind them of that marvelous Christian principle of our spirituality, in which suffering when loved as a countenance of Jesus crucified and forsaken is changed into joy.

Now let's add a word to all who are living this Christmas day in serenity and joy.

Knowing that anyone who walks on the path of God cannot escape from suffering, let's wish that everyone may know how to welcome every small or great suffering that they encounter with great love, to present it as a gift for the Child Jesus who is born today, just as the three kings offered their gifts. It will be the best incense, the best gold, and the best myrrh that we could place in the manger.

May this be our Christmas and also our commitment for the next two weeks: to share in all the sufferings of our neighbors who are most under trial, and offer our own sufferings to the Child Jesus.

December 25, 1986

...by the same author from New City Press

Journey

Life is a journey. For the believer it is a pilgrimage to God, to the fullness of life in him. The author and the members of the Focolare with whom she originally shared these thoughts during periodic conference calls, have chosen to make this pilgrimage together. This book is a kind of log of their journey, and at the same time a gold mine of spiritual encouragement and practical suggestions for anyone who has set out on this "Holy Journey."
0-911782-51-6, 151 pp

Diary 1964/65

In addition to the story of events and encounters at the time of Vatican II, this is a journey of the soul. These are the innermost thoughts and reflections of a wayfarer constantly listening to the Holy Spirit, constantly sharing the spirituality of unity based on Jesus in the midst.
0-911782-55-9, 176 pp

Meditations

6th printing

Already translated into fourteen languages, this book is a collection of 54 meditations which are based on a profound experience of living the Gospel. Since 1943, Chiara Lubich's experience, intuitions, and understandings have inspired millions throughout the world to live and work for unity.
0-911782-20-6, 134 pp

Unity and Jesus Forsaken

"...In our contemporary society, so often devoid of simplicity and directness, the Focolare movement is a breath of fresh air. Without being simplistic or reductionistic, Lubich challenges her associates to focus on Jesus forsaken as the model for unity and the key to living a life of joy.... There can be no unity without a lived theology of the cross."
Robert Morneau, Auxiliary Bishop of Green Bay, Emmanuel Magazine
0-911782-53-2, 105 pp

When Did We See You, Lord?

The extraordinary dignity of every person, each individual's capacity for the infinite, and the need to discover God in our fellow human beings are some of the recurring themes here. The question, "Who is my neighbor?" is answered in the light of the Old and New Testaments, and in terms of our relationship with other Christians, with members of other religions, and with nonbelievers. The author describes how, by loving others, people can move from lives that are meaningless and empty to lives that are full and, in a real sense, divine.
0-911782-34-6, 134 pp

The Eucharist

"In four concise talks, the author gives the great plan of God for communicating life through Jesus and the Eucharist, which has always been the heart of the Church in its work of divinization of man in incorporating man into Christ to build that one body and one spirit." *Liguorian*
0-911782-30-3, 93 pp

May They All Be One

This book is dedicated to the increasing numbers of people interested in knowing about the events and ideas that contributed to the birth and growth of the Focolare. The principal setting for this brief account is World War II. The story is told by its main protagonist, Chiara Lubich.
0-911782-46-X, 96 pp

Servants of All

"...This loving presence of Jesus in the Church as a whole, and in its ministers (the hierarchy) — which is presented as a reflection of the life of the Trinity, an extension of Heaven's life on earth — is a dominant theme which pervades the book, giving it a distinctive quality." "...A careful reading of the various topics will immediately reveal that Chiara's approach is neither superficial or dull, but profound and alive." (from the foreword by Federico Didonet, Bishop of Rio Grande)
0-911782-05-2, 176 pp

Unity - Our Adventure
The Focolare Movement

In these pages we will tell the story of an adventure: that of the Focolare. It is an adventure that is lived out everyday and has unfolded in the course of time through people whose only strength is an immense trust in God. This publication intends to offer a rapid panorama of the Focolare's spirituality and history.
0-911782-56-7, 80 pp, 40 color/47 b/w photographs, hardbound